Greyhound SCENICRUISER

Flagship of the Fleet

TOM MCNALLY & FRED RAYMAN

Iconografix

Iconografix
1830A Hanley Road
Hudson, Wisconsin 54016 USA

Library of Congress Control Number: 2013933480

ISBN-13: 978-1-58388-301-3
ISBN-10: 1-58388-301-0

13 14 15 16 17 18 6 5 4 3 2 1

Printed in The United States of America

Contents

ACKNOWLEDGEMENTS

We are thankful to the following people for their contributions and support: John Adams, Bob Beard, Kyle Brandt, Don Coffin, Bryan Cooper, Fred Dunikoski, Peter Govorchin, Roy Hall, Andy Henderson, Andy Henderson, Jr., Jon Hobein, Jim Husing, Bruce Korusek, Loring Lawrence, Alex Lock, Bill Luke, Skip Malone, Hari McNally, Ron Medaglia, Jim Michaud, Dave Millhouser, Peter Newgard, John Oakman, David Pagel, Doc Rushing, Joe Semmes, Richard Silagi, Ron Van Kleech, John Vickers, Robert Winter III.

DEDICATION

For Joey: From one big kid to one little kid – May we always share our passion for playing with toys – No matter how old we get! I love you. *Daddy-o*

Introduction:

Which items in our culture genuinely deserve to be described as iconic, nostalgic, antique, or Americana? What attributes must an object possess to be described by these words? First, *iconic* should refer to something that is familiar, enduring, and universally recognizable. That item should break all traditions and it should be superior when considered alongside everything else. An icon should be unique and it should be something around which people have built fond memories. It should be a much praised object not standing for itself, but rather the collective experiences of an era—something that folks can look at and say out loud, "Hey, I remember that." These beloved items so thoroughly permeate the American culture that they blend into the background and become part of our daily lives. When we deem things iconic, they have naturally become part of history and have earned a permanent status of importance to us.

The term *nostalgic* should describe a true longing or yearning for a particular period of time or the "good old days." The feeling can be spurred on by something that reminds us of an item, person, or event from the past. When this happens, we usually recall things in a happy, almost idyllic, manner.

Americana can sometimes be intertwined with nostalgia and it relates to items that evoke a sense of history and folklore as it relates to the United States.

True antiques are timeless and they have had some impact on history. Antiques always have some inherent lasting value.

One such object is a particular intercity coach, one that exemplifies these sentiments—the almost universally adored Greyhound PD-4501 Scenicruiser bus, built by the GM Corporation during 1954-'56. After nearly 60 years, people do not stop talking about this particular model of bus. Its popularity, even today, is almost cult-like. Throughout the history of intercity coaches in the U.S., there have not been more toys, advertising pieces, souvenirs, or memorabilia centered on any other bus. When you talk about the famous Greyhound Scenicruiser, you talk about calendars, menus, postcards, timetables, ashtrays—you name it, and Greyhound used it. The Scenicruiser starred in several movies, was featured on record album covers, and appeared on endless TV shows through the years. If you are of a certain age, you will recall that this was the preferred mode of long-distance travel for most Americans for nearly two decades.

I am lucky enough to own a restored Greyhound Scenicruiser and when I take it out for an occasional spin, without fail, some other motorist or pedestrian will stop in their tracks to have a look. It always amazes me—the immediate reaction of excitement that an old bus can evoke from people. Strangers on the street, people you have never met, drop what they are doing to look at and talk to me about the coach. I get real joy and satisfaction in seeing the surprised, stunned, almost gleeful expression on their faces. Sometimes, when a person sees the bus, they have what I describe as an instant flashback. You can see them returning to a simpler, happier, and possibly more optimistic time in their minds. It is obvious: the sight of the coach immediately brings back some long forgotten memory. Whether they remember riding a Scenicruiser as vacationing children, military people, businessmen, college students, or Greyhound drivers—they all have fond memories and stories of riding the bus and I love to hear them all!

Tom McNally

Chapter 1: Prototypes

GX-2

In an effort to increase passenger and luggage capacity, in 1948 the Greyhound Motors and Supply subsidiary in Chicago began working on an experimental, hand-built, futuristic prototype called the GX-2 or Scenicruiser. GM supplied a partially assembled PD-4151 to get them started. The styling of this lone example was created by world-famous industrial designers Raymond Loewy and Associates, and it marked a new era in highway travel. Loewy had created endless familiar identities for Americans, which include the original Coca-Cola bottle, the Shell Oil logo, the Lucky Strike cigarette package, and many more. The GX-2 began as a 35-foot long, single-rear-axle, full-scale model, but it was later converted to an unprecedented length of 40 feet. This strikingly handsome coach was a deck-and-a-half monocoque design that ultimately used tandem rear axles. The rearmost axle was the drive, and the intermediate was the non-powered tag. The rear drive axle had dual wheels, while the tag axle ran single wheels. GX-2 was equipped with a single, transversely mounted in-line GM 6-71 diesel engine, a manual four-speed transmission, and power steering. This concept coach served as a test vehicle during the developmental stage for many drive train combinations, and proved revolutionary in transportation innovation. It used conventional steel springs, but it was instrumental in the eventual design of air-ride suspension. The GX-2 seated 10 on the lower deck and 33 on the upper deck, with a rear lounge similar to those on a train observation car of the day. The lavatory was at the foot of the stairs on the lower level, on the right side (opposite of where the restroom eventually was located on the production Scenicruiser that followed). This streamlined beauty featured air conditioning, six glass skylights, whitewall tires, a public-address system, and even windshield wipers on the rear window. The design was said to be reminiscent of vista-dome railroad coaches of the past. Oversized side-sash windows were included for improved passenger sightseeing. In time, the roof-mounted destination sign was moved below the windshield. The coach was completed in June of 1949, and embarked on a four-year promotional tour of several state capitals to persuade lawmakers to increase their present 35-foot state limits to permit the use of 40-foot buses. The tour was a success, the state regulations became uniform, and Greyhound got permission to go ahead with their 40-foot coaches. After the completion of the publicity tours, the GX-2 entered revenue service for Great Lakes Greyhound Lines as fleet number G-7483. The bus was retired in 1957, and sold to The Ralph Marterie Orchestra in 1958. It was sold again to The Blue Ridge Quartet of Spartanburg, South Carolina. Unfortunately, rumors exist that the GX-2 eventually ended up in a Nashville, Tennessee, junkyard, and was most likely destroyed.

The GX-2 prototype appears in an advertisement for Pittsburgh Plate Glass Company in the November 1949 issue of *Bus Transportation* magazine. *Tom McNally collection*

GX-2 lower deck interior view toward rear of the coach. The restroom was at the foot of the stairs on the right. *Don Coffin collection*

Driver/Engineer Ray Kramer with GX-2. *Don Coffin collection*

GX-2 had ample, large side windows for sightseeing. Note the wrap-around upper deck windshield. *Don Coffin collection*

Mock-up

After the creation of the GX-2, a full scale mock-up styling concept model of the Scenicruiser was built by GM, in Pontiac, Michigan. It shared many of the same styling cues with the GM PD-4104, only with a deck-and-a-half design instead of a single-level coach. The overall look of this faux bus represented how the production Scenicruisers would appear when they were built.

EXP-331

The Truck and Coach Division of the GM Corporation built a second experimental prototype in 1953 known as EXP-331. It was handmade in the Truck and Coach facilities in Pontiac, Michigan. The bus was built with almost the same exact details as those on the full-sized mock-up. This coach served as a final model for the manufacturing platform for all 1,000 production Scenicruisers that were produced. It carried the original paint scheme that became standard for the Cruiser. EXP-331 was built with an emergency exit door on the left side to comply with existing New Jersey state law. This was the only 4501 ever built with this exit door. With the addition of emergency kick-out roof hatches (skylights) and side windows, the need for an extra escape door was eliminated, and it never went into actual production. This experimental coach was also the only Scenicruiser to ever have a spotlight factory-installed (on the A pillar). In 1956, after engineering tests were completed, and after the full production run of cruisers was finished, EXP-331 was refurbished and delivered as PD4501-1001 to Atlantic Greyhound Lines as A-2267. In a strange turn of events, in a sense, this bus could be considered the first and last 4501 built. At some point, the E-door and spotlight were removed by Greyhound, possibly during the 1961-'62 rebuild. Eventually it was renumbered as 5399, and was still listed on Greyhound's roster as late as 1974. Over time, it was sold to several different private charter companies, the last of which was Ridgely Coach of Washington D.C., in the mid 1980s. Upon the advice of Fred Rayman, Gordon Phalzgraf (a private collector, from Belpre, Ohio) acquired the prototype in 1985. It was stored indoors, preserved as original, and then resold again in 2008 to Tom McNally of Peoria, Illinois. In the future, PD4501-1001 will undergo a complete restoration.

View forward of the GX-2 upper deck interior, including several of the ceiling skylights. *Don Coffin collection*

Windshield wipers on the rear window can be seen in this early promotional photo of the GX-2 Scenicruiser. *Don Coffin collection*

The beautiful, flowing lines of the experimental GX-2 with its roof-mounted destination sign. The sign would eventually be moved below the front windshields. *Don Coffin collection*

GX-2 upper deck interior view toward rear of the coach. *Don Coffin collection*

In this promotional photo, passengers enjoy the lounge area in the rear of the GX-2. *Don Coffin collection*

The GX-2 prototype under construction in Chicago, circa 1948. *Don Coffin collection*

Panoramic view forward from upper deck windshields on the GX-2 prototype. *Don Coffin collection*

Prototype GX-2 hand-built by Greyhound Lines in Chicago circa 1949. *Don Coffin collection*

A promotional photograph of the GX-2 experimental coach. Notice the gleaming Goodyear whitewall tires. *Don Coffin collection*

The Blue Ridge Quartet of Spartanburg, South Carolina, featured their tour bus (GX-2) on their 1965 southern gospel record release of "Passing Thru." *Tom McNally collection*

Greyhound promotional advertising booklet featuring the amenities of the GX-2 Scenicruiser. *Fred Rayman collection*

An advertisement for Edwards side sash windows from *Bus Transportation* magazine (October 1949 issue) featuring the GX-2. *Tom McNally collection*

The Blue Ridge Quartet on the road in Miami, Florida, in December of 1964. *Roy Hall collection*

GMC experimental model builders under the direction of F.R. Eichner, Senior Engineer, put the finishing touches on their exact mock-up of the Scenicruiser. Note this paint scheme never saw actual production. *Don Coffin collection*

The full-sized model had a wooden skeleton, and was hollow with no interior detail. The replica even wears a 1953 Michigan Manufacturer license plate. Note the left side high-mount outside mirror, a styling cue from the GM PD-4104, which never made production on the Scenicruiser. *Don Coffin collection*

EXP-331, the experimental prototype built in 1953 and photographed in Pontiac, Michigan, just prior to being delivered as the last Scenicruiser off the assembly line to Atlantic Greyhound Lines as fleet number A-2267 and serial number PD4501-1001. *Don Coffin collection*

PD4501-1001 (A-2267) showing off its left side emergency exit door. The rear side hinged engine-access doors with twin swing-out mounted radiators can be clearly seen in this factory photo. PD4501-1001 was delivered to Atlantic Greyhound Lines in Charleston, West Virginia, on July 18, 1956. *Don Coffin collection*

Pennsylvania Greyhound Lines P5539 (PD4501-403) in the original 1954 livery. *Bruce Korusek collection*

Experimental prototype EXP-331 during construction and Engineering testing in Pontiac, Michigan, circa 1953. Note the four individual windshield wiper arms and driver's spot-light; both features never went on the production Scenicruisers. *Don Coffin collection*

"Detroit Express" reads the destination sign on T-903 (PD4501-124). Note the early Trico (3 blades) windshield wipers. This is one of six Scenicruisers delivered new to Teche Greyhound Lines of New Orleans, Louisiana. *Don Coffin collection*

Atlantic Greyhound Lines A2204 (PD4501-014). *Bruce Korusek collection*

A vintage placemat made of paper from a Greyhound Post House Restaurant. *Tom McNally collection*

some examples of memorabilia: a felt pennant, 1964 New York World's Fair matchbook cover, 1961 calendar, a York, Pennsylvania, Greyhound advertising ashtray and an advertising folder for "Greyhound Florida Circle Tours." *Tom McNally collection*

Classic Scenicruiser tin toy made in Japan. *Fred Rayman collection*

An early tin toy depot produced by Marx toy company and two Tootsie toy die cast Scenicruisers. *Tom McNally collection*

The original twin engine style tailgate access doors can be seen on Atlantic Greyhound Lines A2200 (PD4501-003) and A2202 (PD4501-012). *Bruce Korusek collection*

Atlantic Greyhound Lines A2201 (PD4501-011). *Bruce Korusek collection*

Atlantic Greyhound Lines A2204 (PD4501-014) alongside a Hansom cab in New York City circa 1955. The coach was on a special trip for members of the Motor Bus Society. *Bruce Korusek collection*

Pennsylvania Greyhound Lines P5453 (PD4501-029) parked alongside a PD4104 GMC coach. *Bruce Korusek collection*

Easter Greyhound Lines E5545 (PD4501-426). *Bruce Korusek collection*

Atlantic Greyhound Lines A2202 (PD4501-012). *Bruce Korusek collection*

The Saturday Evening Post, January 21, 1956. *Tom McNally collection*

The Saturday Evening Post, September 25, 1955. *Tom McNally collection*

"Every mile a magnificent mile – By Scenicruiser"—Mount Hood, Oregon, calendar (July 1955). *Tom McNally collection*

"Greyhound brings you a new way to hurry home for the Holidays – In Scenicruiser luxury!" *Tom McNally collection*

Nice close-up of the 1954 interior driver's compartment with original Johnson-bar manual park brake lever to left of the driver's seat, and Hi-Lo transmission gear shift knob switch. Note the dash includes gauges for the original dual engines. *Don Coffin collection*

P5548 (PD4501-017) belonged to Pennsylvania Greyhound Lines; in this photo it wears a state of Ohio 1955 license plate. *Don Coffin collection*

Chapter 2:
1954-1956
The Flagship of the Fleet Arrives

After the creation of two prototypes, an endless engineering effort, and several years of testing, the big day had arrived. The wait was finally over. The much anticipated arrival of the brand-new Greyhound Scenicruiser mesmerized crowds at a giant unveiling ceremony held on July 14, 1954, in Pontiac, Michigan. Greyhound President Orville Caesar, general manager of GM Coach Division, Phillip J. Monaghan, and Governor of Michigan, Gerhard Mennen Williams, were a few of many anxious onlookers on hand to take part in this historic moment. The press also watched as Scenicruiser C-675 (serial number 006) burst through a giant paper poster covering the doorway of GM factory building 34. During the festivities, a traditional bottle of champagne was broken on the front bumper of F-701 (serial number 002) by Mrs. America, Wanda Jennings, of St. Louis, Missouri. Greyhound and General Motors officials toured the Scenicruiser assembly line following the ceremonies.

In the fall of 1954, Greyhound President Orville Caesar was asked about how the new coaches were doing. He said, "Our new Scenicruiser, which was first placed in service in September, has met with the enthusiastic approval of the public wherever it has been used. We first inaugurated service between New York and Miami and as these great coaches came off the assembly line, we added them to other principal routes until most of our important lines are now operated, in part at least, with Scenicruiser equipment. To date, about 150 of them have been placed in service with another 350 of the initial order to be delivered. They will continue to be placed in service on our principal divisions as they are delivered to us."

The Scenicruiser was designated as model PD-4501. The P is for parlor, D is for diesel, 45 is the original seating capacity (before the restroom was included), and 01 represents the first in the series. Just like the GX-2 before, the classic 1954 production version (exclusively for Greyhound) was the work of legendary designer Raymond Loewy. It was the very first 40-foot intercity coach in regular production, and included standard air conditioning, power steering, restroom, public address system, and air-ride suspension. The deck-and-a-half design included a record 345 cubic feet of baggage storage inside two huge under-floor compartments.

With gleaming fluted aluminum siding, the coach was eight feet wide, and seated 43 passengers. The coach stood about 11 feet and 2 inches in height, and weighed about 30,000 pounds empty (40,000 or more fully loaded). The body design remained monocoque (frameless). Power was provided by a pair of four-cylinder (150 HP each, 4-71 GM Diesel) engines that were mounted next to each other (lying on their sides) on a single cradle for easy removal. Twin engines were necessary because one single engine, powerful enough for the large coach, did not yet exist. The two engines were connected together by a fluid coupling. Only the right-side engine had a starter, air conditioning compressor, air compressor for brakes, and the air-ride suspension. The left-hand engine was automatically started through the fluid coupling arrangement. The ability for the coach to operate on one engine in case of emergencies was advertised heavily, but in fact was not possible. The three-speed manual Spicer transmission used a two-speed hydraulic clutch that supplied six forward gears. The hydraulic clutch was engaged and disengaged by an electric solenoid operated by a foot treadle on the left side of the steering column in the driver's compartment. The clutch speed was controlled by a small horizontally mounted hi-low electrical switch on the gearshift lever. A mid-production change replaced the electrically activated clutch to traditional mechanical linkage on all the Scenicruisers; this was due to an overheating of these solenoids when left engaged (in traffic) for long periods of time. The same three-axle design was retained from the concept models; however, the trailing axle was the rearmost and the drive now in the middle. For improved traction and load capacity, both rear axles ran dual wheels. Originally, industry non-standard 19-inch tires were fitted to curb theft of tires and rims by thieves.

Trico windshield wipers (with three wiper blades) were standard, until a mid-production change was made to pantograph-style wipers to improve effectiveness. The much touted air-conditioning system was said to be capable of completely changing the air within the bus every 40 seconds. The Cruisers were built with four glass skylights (three upstairs and one downstairs). The skylights were eventually blanked out by white paint on the exterior and opaque contact paper on the interior. Covering the skylights was done to appease passengers who complained of being woken up as the coach passed under bright streetlights at night. This was also done to alleviate excess heat from daytime sunlight. One of the more peculiar details of the coach exterior was a small red "circle R" decal located on each side, above the teardrop window, toward the front on the upper deck. Apparently, this was Greyhound's method of displaying their registered trademark for the unique dual-level coach design.

The interior was finished throughout in an attractive light yellow color known as "Wheat Harvest Shadow." The lower-level upholstery was done in solid gold-colored fabric with tiny blue and white accents, and did not include vinyl edges or backing on seats. Individual reclining seats included headrests covered in white cloth, armrests covered in black, and an adjustable footrest for each passenger. The interior upholstered side panels, below the windows, were yellow as well. On the lower-level of the coach, the aluminum edge panels on the seats (below the armrest) were painted Greyhound blue. These same panels on the upper-level were painted bright red. The upper-level seats featured black cloth with the same small flecks of blue and white, again with no vinyl edges or back. The driver's seat and entry door vinyl hinge cover were done in matching yellow. The vinyl floors were furbished in white color throughout. The very large Edwards side-sash windows with Solex green tint provided reduced glare and breathtaking panoramic views. Other amenities included personal vents or "cigarette smoke evacuators" as they were labeled, and a reading lamp was mounted above each passenger. In addition, ashtrays and hat storage hooks were attached to the rear of each seat. As a reminder for drivers, there was a small air-operated warning sign mounted in the sun-visor area that was normally concealed. The sign would trigger if one of the baggage-bin doors was left open. The two-inch round "wig-wag" caution read "STOP – DOOR OPEN – RESET."

The initial order from Greyhound was for 500 units to be produced. In order to lower manufacturing costs, 500 more coaches were manufactured. The Scenicruiser cost about $50,000 each when new. Upon completion at a rate of two per day in Pontiac, Michigan, coaches were driven the 80 miles to the Greyhound shop in Toledo, Ohio, for installation of passenger seats, air conditioning components, and final adjustments. The building of the 1,001 Scenicruisers lasted from August of 1954 through June of 1956. Their popularity was instant, and they soon ascended to the status of flagship of the Greyhound fleet.

Under the Sherman Antitrust Act of 1890, the US Department of Justice filed suit against GM in 1956. That office claimed that GM held a monopoly on the US bus market, due to their 84% market share at the time. The suit never went to trial, but part of the final agreement, which came in 1965, no longer allowed General Motors to enter into exclusive-design contracts with Greyhound or other companies. This, alongside a lawsuit that Greyhound filed against GM, was the beginning of the end for their long-standing relationship.

A newly manufactured Scenicruiser appears in the July 4th parade Detroit, Michigan, in 1954. *Fred Rayman collection*

Western Greyhound lines P-2433 (PD4501-454) in Sacramento, California, circa 1960. *Tom McNally collection*

As new Scenicruiser coaches are paraded past the crowd in Pontiac, Michigan, Orville Caesar (President of the Greyhound Corp.) addresses the audience on July 14, 1954. *Tom McNally collection*

Pennsylvania Greyhound Lines P-5446 (PD4501-001). *Roy Hall collection*

The traditional bottle of champagne is broken as Mrs. America, Wanda Jennings, christens Florida Greyhound Lines F-701 (PD4501-002) in Pontiac, Michigan, on July 14, 1954. *Tom McNally collection*

The destination sign on Central Greyhound Lines of New York C-677 (PD4501-032) reads: Chicago Express. Note the Greyhound Lines stake truck parked in the background of the Chicago Greyhound garage. *Roy Hall collection*

Atlantic Greyhound Lines A-2204 (PD4501-014). *Roy Hall collection*

Atlantic Greyhound Lines A-2200 (PD4501-003). *Roy Hall collection*

Orville S. Caesar (left), President of the Greyhound Corp., with Mrs. America Wanda Jennings, and E.P. Crenshaw, Sales Manager of General Motors Coach Division, at the Scenicruiser unveiling in Pontiac, Michigan, on July 14, 1954. *Tom McNally collection*

Great Lakes Greyhound Lines G-7250 (PD4501-292) on publicity tour display circa 1954. *Fred Rayman collection*

Central Greyhound Lines of New York C-675 (PD4501-006) emerges from GM factory building 34 on July 14, 1954. *Tom McNally collection*

Eastern Greyhound Lines E-5490 (PD4501-568) stops at a toll booth along the Massachusetts Turnpike. *Fred Rayman collection*

Greyhound Bus Station in Jacksonville, Florida. *Tom McNally collection*

This postcard is postmarked 1960 and reads: "Greyhound Post House – Gilman, Illinois. 'City of the Cross Roads' Located at the intersection of U.S. Highway 24, 45, 54 this up-to-date and air conditioned Restaurant serves excellent food for the traveler. Open 24 hours a day – Every day in the year." *Tom McNally collection*

Waco, Texas, Greyhound Bus Terminal and Greyhound Post House Cafeteria located in downtown Waco. *Tom McNally collection*

This postcard reads: "Stephen Foster Restaurant – At the Suwannee River, on Route 98 – 27 & 19 at Fanning Springs, Florida. Famous for Suwannee River catfish & hushpuppies, open 24 hours daily. Owner and operated by Mr. & Mrs. G.K. Page." *Tom McNally collection*

Pennsylvania Greyhound Lines P-5446 (PD4501-001) on display at the Capitol Greyhound Terminal, West 50th Street, New York City, circa 1954. *Don Coffin collection*

This promotional advertising photograph shows the lower interior of the Scenicruiser. *Don Coffin collection*

Pacific Greyhound Lines K2208 (PD4501-093). Note the original location of the twin-engine air intake screens in the beltline, at the left rear corner. *Don Coffin collection*

Northwest Greyhound Lines Y-700 (PD4501-082). *Don Coffin collection*

Pennsylvania Greyhound Lines P-5446 (PD4501-001). *Roy Hall collection*

This 1955 advertisement proclaimed, "See exactly what you get – when you choose Greyhound low-cost luxury." *Tom McNally collection*

With a beautiful Florida sunset on Lake Maggiore, this 1954 calendar stated: "The Scenicruiser begins a new era in travel." *Tom McNally collection*

The Saturday Evening Post 1955 advertisement. *Tom McNally collection*

Pennsylvania Greyhound Lines P-5446 (PD4501- 001). *Roy Hall collection*

Pennsylvania Greyhound Lines P-5446 (PD4501-001). *Roy Hall collection*

A pair of Scenicruisers in the second paint scheme (Scenicruiser Service) parked at the Seattle, Washington, Greyhound terminal and Post House restaurant circa 1961. *Bryan Cooper collection*

1954 Greyhound Corporation Stockholders annual report. *Fred Rayman collection*

An elegantly dressed passenger poses with a San Francisco bound Scenicruiser. *Don Coffin collection*

Overland Greyhound Lines O-1701 (PD4501-038) in Evanston, Illinois, on August 27, 1954. *Fred Rayman collection*

In this photo of Atlantic Greyhound Lines A-2215 (PD4501-177) the "baggage bin door open" warning flag can be seen deployed at the top of the driver's side windshield. This was to remind drivers that the bin door must be closed prior to departure. The original two-piece hinged driver's window can also be seen. *Don Coffin collection*

WGL P-2400 (PD4501-007) on a Los Angeles to Chicago schedule stops at the Hotel Dixon, located in Dixon, Illinois, on July 7, 1958. *Loring M. Lawrence collection*

"Greyhound—Every Mile A Magnificent Mile!" *Collier's* magazine (April 1955 issue). *Tom McNally collection*

Grand Canyon National Park calendar (October 1955) stating: "Every highway a strip of velvet – by Scenicruiser." *Tom McNally collection*

Manhattan skyline, including the U.N. building; note the lack of a restroom on this coach. It has been touched-up incorrectly by artists, as passengers are sitting on lower level left where the Lavatory would be (June 1956 calendar). *Tom McNally collection*

"Explore this amazing America in low-cost luxury," proclaimed this Indian scene ad. *Tom McNally collection*

Samsonite luggage and Greyhound share this advertisement featuring June Allyson and Dick Powell. *Tom McNally collection*

A Scenicruiser emerges from a side street in Washington D.C. on March 25, 1955. *Roy Hall collection*

This 1:48 scale replica of Evansville, Indiana's Greyhound terminal was modeled by MTH, with a Russian-built St. Petersburg Tram Collection 1:48 scale replica PD-4501 parked at the curb. At the docks on the right are a Corgi die-cast Scenicruiser, and a MTH-built die-cast PD-3751 GMC Silversides in the background. *Tom McNally collection*

Central Greyhound Lines of New York C-675 (PD4501-006) promotional photo at the Cranbrook Institute of Science located in Detroit, Michigan. *Jon Hobein collection*

The dash-mounted tachograph can be seen in this photo of Eastern Greyhound Lines E-5495 (PD4501-504). A tachograph is a device fitted to a vehicle that automatically records speed, time, and distance on wax coated paper discs. Eastern Greyhound Lines was among few divisions to utilize tachographs as they were required by New Jersey state law. Note the early Coca-Cola truck in the background of this New York City street scene. *Roy Hall collection*

Eastern Greyhound Lines E-5475 (PD4501-202) St. Louis Express. *Roy Hall collection*

Southwestern Greyhound Lines S-126 (PD4501-264). *Don Coffin collection*

The destination sign reads "New York Express" on Pennsylvania Greyhound Lines P-5532 (PD4501-334). *Don Coffin collection*

Southwestern Greyhound Lines S-157 (PD4501-498) boards, bound for Laredo, Texas. *Fred Rayman collection*

The destination sign reads "Washington Express" on this Atlantic Greyhound Lines A2238 (PD4501-849). The coach wears the second paint scheme with the "Scenicruiser Service" slogan on the beltline in this 1959 photograph. *Fred Rayman collection*

The destination was New York for this Easter Greyhound Lines E-1096 (PD4501-470) photographed in Montreal, circa 1959. *Fred Rayman collection*

Eastern Greyhound Lines E-5517 (PD4501-297). *Bruce Korusek collection*

"Scenicruiser service" was provided by Eastern Greyhound Lines E-1129 (PD4501-887), shown here in Montreal on April 14, 1958. *Fred Rayman collection*

Eastern Greyhound Lines E-5520 (PD4501-300) photographed in July of 1960. *Bruce Korusek collection*

Shown are some souvenirs, including: Guy Lombardo and his Royal Canadians record (Eastern Greyhound Lines E-5558 PD4501-563), a fantasy based Japanese tin toy, a ceramic Scenicruiser keepsake from Lake Charles, Louisiana, a faux chocolate bar used for sales display at a Greyhound Post House Restaurant, and a Post House coffee cup and saucer. *Tom McNally collection*

Pacific Greyhound Lines K-2285 (PD4501-579) appears on this mailing envelope that contained a die-cut paper Scenicruiser model kit. Greyhound co-sponsored the Steve Allen Show which appeared on NBC-TV every Sunday night. The variety show even had a real live Greyhound dog mascot named "Steverino." *Tom McNally collection*

Metcalf Bros. official Greyhound driver's uniform fabric samples, the 4501R operating manual issued after the 1961/1962 Marmon-Herrington rebuild, a pocket calendar, and a tin toy. *Tom McNally collection*

This vintage 36-inch plastic Scenicruiser model used as a display in Greyhound terminals. *Fred Rayman collection*

A classic advertisement from *The Saturday Evening Post*. "Fred Waring and his Pennsylvanians go Greyhound on a 25,000 mile tour!" *Tom McNally collection*

Central Greyhound Lines C-675 (PD4501-006) appears in this *Saturday Evening Post* advertisement. "Mrs. America goes Greyhound." *Tom McNally collection*

Florida Greyhound Lines F-701 (PD4501-002) and F-702 (PD4501-009). *Roy Hall collection*

"Express" Scenicruiser in the original 1954 livery. *Roy Hall collection*

Central Greyhound Lines of New York C-7285 (PD4501-653). *Roy Hall collection*

"Biscayne Limited" Florida Greyhound Lines F-703 (PD4501-010). *Roy Hall collection*

Chapter 3: Greyhound Promotions, Marketing & Advertising

In the fall of 1954, Greyhound supplied Fred Waring and the Pennsylvanians a brand new Scenicruiser to launch a 200-city North American band tour. The world-famous radio and TV legend, Fred Waring, scheduled a 25,000-mile tour across the USA and Canada. The bus selected for this historic charter was P-5446 (serial number PD4501-001), from the Pennsylvania Greyhound Lines and was operated by the same company driver (John Tyrell of Philadelphia) for some seven months, and covered all 48 states as well as portions of Canada. This was a highly unusual lengthy charter, and may have been Greyhound's longest charter ever. The tour was highlighted in a Greyhound Lines advertisement that appeared in *The Saturday Evening Post.* Advertising efforts for the Scenicruiser were top-notch during the 1950s and 1960s. The Steve Allen Show, which aired every Sunday night on NBC television, was sponsored by Greyhound; more specifically, it was directly tied to the Scenicruiser. In a joint effort to promote the Steve Allen Show and the bus company, a die-cut paper model kit of the Scenicruiser was distributed for kids. A cardboard 45 RPM record bearing Scenicruiser artwork and Greyhound logos were also made available as promotional items to Steve Allen show fans. Images of the world-famous bus turned up everywhere. Guy Lombardo and His Royal Canadians, a band, used a creative head-on shot of Eastern Greyhound Lines E-5558 (PD4501-563) on the cover of their 1957 "Lombardoland" record. The opening scene of *Rat Race*, a 1960 movie starring Tony Curtis, almost appeared to be a five-minute advertisement for Greyhound with tremendous shots of Eastern Greyhound Lines E-5611 (PD4501-819). Alfred Hitchcock's thriller *North by Northwest* (1959), starring Cary Grant, also included a brief scene including Pacific Greyhound Lines K-2332 (PD4501-832). Western Greyhound Lines 8066 (PD4501-437) was also used in *Breakfast at Tiffany's* (1961), starring Audrey Hepburn.

In the fall of 1961, Greyhound teamed with Pan American World Airways to promote travel to the USA. A Scenicruiser (PD4501-426), Eastern Greyhound Lines 4374, was shipped to Europe to embark on a multi-country 30-day tour to advertise Greyhound's "Visit the USA for $99" campaign. The coach received a special paint job that included both the Greyhound name and the Pan Am logo. It was outfitted with interchangeable banners affixed to the side that were printed in the appropriate language for the country it happened to be visiting. The bus was reportedly well received all over Europe, and the program was a large success. The same bus was later used in a Reyco brake equipment magazine ad and in an oversized souvenir Greyhound Lines picture postcard.

Another attempt to expand into foreign markets came in the late 1960s. Greyhound's new far-Eastern joint venture was known as Korea Greyhound. A total of approximately 40 coaches were overhauled in San Francisco, painted in the red-stripe livery, and shipped to Korea. This new overseas fleet included both PD-4104s and PD-4501s.

PD4501-514 Greyhound Corporate Transport

In 1956, Arthur S. Genet, the new president of Greyhound, removed Great Lakes Greyhound Lines G-7262 (PD4501-514) from revenue service. This bus was chosen to be Greyhound's corporate transport limo, and would lend itself as an office-on-wheels for a three-month trip. From October to December 1956, Greyhound's President embarked on a 10,000-mile public relations journey to inspect several Greyhound Facilities throughout the country. The coach was reassigned the fleet number GC-13. This particular Scenicruiser had a drumhead sign installed on the rear of the coach, similar to those found on trains of the day. On one occasion, the bus was taken to the Tootsietoy headquarters in Chicago, Illinois, for inspection. The toy company had plans to manufacture a die-cast model of the already famous Greyhound.

When Fred W. Ackerman took the reins of Greyhound in 1959, GC-13 was then leased to the Anheuser-Busch Company. This would be the first time when a Scenicruiser was used for any non-Greyhound activity. The bus was modified to promote Anheuser's new Busch beer. The seats on the lower level were removed to make way for beer refrigerators. Card tables, individual captain's chairs, and a rear lounge area were among added amenities on the upper level. Passengers were also treated to a kitchenette, serving area with hot and cold water, and the standard restroom on the lower level. The Anheuser, as it was called, had a dedicated Greyhound employed driver at the wheel while it was on tour. Interestingly enough, the bus had the Greyhound name only in small letters on the baggage-bin doors. It sported Anheuser-Busch lettering and logos in prominent fashion. PD4501-514 eventually reentered Greyhound's regular revenue fleet as Central Greyhound Lines C-7262, and it went on to serve for several more years.

Greyhound Personalized Radio Service

Around 1962, Greyhound decided to enhance its East Coast service to Florida by installing an individually controlled Motorola AM radio at every passenger seat aboard a limited number of Scenicruisers. Greyhound also operated through-service between Montreal and Florida, and these coaches were also fitted with personalized radios. It is believed that from 50 to 60 buses in total were adapted for radio reception. Chrome consoles, one for each seat, were installed along the underside of the overhead luggage racks. Each console contained a station selector, volume dial and headphone plug. The center rectangle of each console displayed the Greyhound name and logo plus the words "Personalized Radio Service." Somewhat inconspicuously cast into one side of the console was the Motorola name. Earphones were connected by a cord into a jack on the console. Above each console, bolted to the floor of the overhead luggage rack, was a chromed tuning module. These modules created somewhat of an obstruction for articles placed in the luggage racks. The master radio receiver was located in the compartment located just behind the left front wheel.

A whip-type antenna, about eight feet long, was mounted in the center of the lower deck roof, and angled back at roughly a 45-degree angle. With a Scenicruiser traveling at speed, the antenna had the habit of tapping incessantly on the upper deck roof! This annoyance was rectified by installing a rubber ball on the aerial at the point of roof contact.

Initially the personalized radios were a free amenity for passengers, but later Greyhound introduced a $1 headset rental fee. It's likely the fee was triggered by the need to recoup some of the maintenance costs of the radio system. They proved troublesome in several respects. The boxes on the baggage shelf were often whacked as passengers stuffed bags and other belongings on the shelves, the wiring was subject to breakage, and the antenna on the roof was often bent or broken when the coaches were washed.

Oddly, Greyhound's venture into personalized radios was barely mentioned in any period advertising. Surprisingly, they were rarely publicized in timetable folders or brochures. Sometime in the late 1960s Greyhound discontinued personalized radios and removed most of the equipment from their Scenicruisers. Small metal block-off plates were installed to hide the holes where former consoles were once mounted. However, not all radios were removed, as a few radio-equipped buses still survive today. And like many other grand experiments, once deemed unsuccessful, they quietly faded away.

Fred Waring and the Pennsylvanians pose with their tour bus P-5446 (PD4501-001) circa 1954. *Don Coffin collection*

Pacific Greyhound Lines K-2334 (PD4501-832) appeared briefly in Alfred Hitchcock's 1959 thriller *North By Northwest* movie. The scene was a desolate crossroads in Indiana, but was actually filmed in East Bakersfield, California. Note the non-standard font on the Hollywood manufactured destination sign, as a western coach would not have Indianapolis readily on its sign scroll. *Bill Luke collection*

Western Greyhound Lines 8078 (PD4501-537) shown in the very rarely seen paint scheme developed to promote escorted tours on Greyhound's own travel agency known as Carrousel. The logo reads "Amazing-America- Vacations," on this one-of-a-kind special edition coach, circa 1963. *FGR collection*

Eastern Greyhound Lines 4531 (PD4501-877) in Nashville, Tennessee, on March 25, 1961. *Loring M. Lawrence collection*

Western Greyhound Lines 8261 (PD4501-523) with its non-standard lettering was photographed in Minneapolis by Bill Luke in 1965. This gold stripe livery coach still bears the moniker of "Scenicruiser Service" that was associated with an earlier 1958-1961 paint scheme. An advertising decal for the 1964/1965 New York World's Fair can also be seen on the entry door. *Bill Luke collection*

The destination sign reads "Twin Cities" on Central Greyhound Lines C-935 (PD4501-194) during a 40-minute lunch stop in Appleton, Wisconsin, on February 14, 1960. This was a Milwaukee-Minneapolis trip via Oshkosh, Appleton, and Stevens Point. *Loring M. Lawrence collection*

Europeans get a chance to experience a Greyhound Scenicruiser. Traveling with Eastern Greyhound Lines 4374 (PD4501-426) across Europe were Greyhound drivers, Pan Am stewardesses, and U.S. Government representatives from the Department of Immigration. Also on board were colorful figures from American history such as cowboys, forest rangers, and American Indians. This photo was taken in Birmingham, England, in 1961. *Jon Hobein collection*

Eastern Greyhound Lines 4374 (PD4501-426) was shipped to Europe for a month-long tour of 13 major cities including London, Amsterdam, Berlin, and Paris. The tour slogan was "See the U.S.A. the Pan Am Greyhound way." *Fred Rayman collection*

Eiffel Tower in Paris, France. *Roy Hall collection*

Eastern Greyhound Lines 4374 (PD4501-426) at the Leaning Tower of Pisa in the fall of 1961. *Roy Hall collection*

Notre Dame Cathedral in Rome, Italy (1961). *Roy Hall collection*

Eastern Greyhound Lines 4374 (PD4501-426) in front of the historic town hall in Frankfort, Germany. *Roy Hall collection*

Eastern Greyhound Lines 4374 (PD4501-426) on display at the The Royal Shakespeare Theatre located in Stratford-upon-Avon, England. Note the flags of various European countries attached to the coach. *Roy Hall collection*

Eastern Greyhound Lines 4374 (PD4501-426) at the The Royal Shakespeare Theatre located in Stratford-upon-Avon, England. *Roy Hall collection*

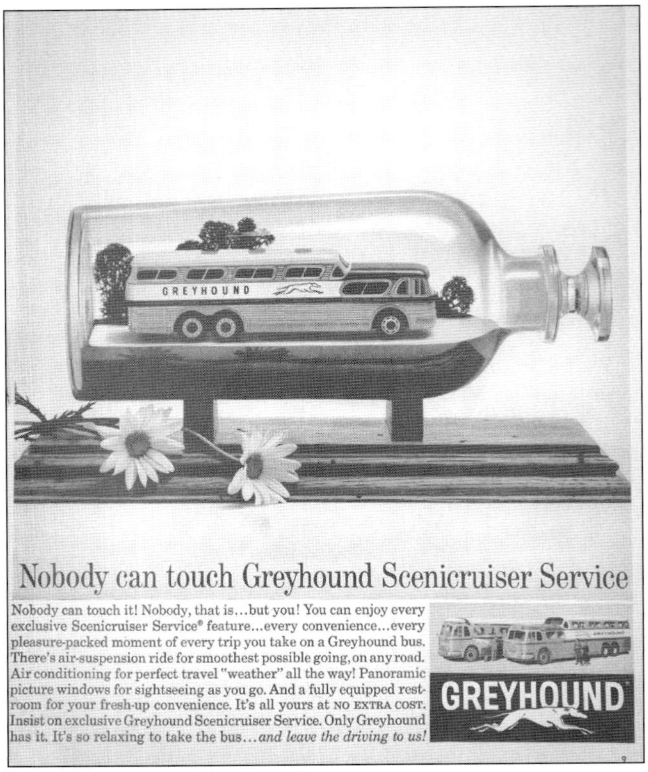

This 1961 advertisement touted, "Nobody can touch Greyhound Scenicruiser Service," with a Scenicruiser in glass bottle. *Tom McNally collection*

Western Greyhound Lines P-2216 (PD4501-255) was used to promote a 1959 Warner Brothers film, *The Young Philadelphians,* starring Paul Newman. The cross-country publicity tour started in Burbank, California, on May 6, 1959, and ended some 3,475 miles later in Philadelphia on May 19, 1959. The 10 star passengers arrived in Philadelphia for the movie premiere, after stopping in 27 cities and 200 towns along the way. *Jon Hobein collection*

Another special paint job adorns Eastern Greyhound Lines E-5627 (PD4501-933) "The Turnpike Express" in New York City, circa 1957. The coach only stopped three times to switch drivers and allowed passengers four rest stops (including a supper break) on the 843-mile journey from New York City to Chicago, Illinois. Rental pillows were available for 30 cents each. These trips were scheduled to last 17 hours and 55 Minutes, and never left the toll roads while en route. Greyhound paid $36.10 in tolls for the entire trip, and charged $20.10 one-way, and $36.20 round trip per passenger. This was one of the very first express travel services to be offered by Greyhound. *Fred Rayman collection*

Southwestern Greyhound Lines S-100 (PD4501-008) with American Airlines Douglas DC-6 Flagship Albany, at Amon Carter airport in Fort Worth, Texas. This was the first Scenicruiser delivered to Southwestern Greyhound Lines. Their home office for Southwestern Greyhound was located in Forth Worth, Texas, at the time. American Airlines named the aircraft in their fleet after big cities on their routes. *Roy Hall collection*

The Greyhound corporate coach parked in front of the historic Savoy-Plaza Hotel in New York City. The Art Deco style hotel had 33 floors and was located at 767 5th Ave. at east 58th Street. It was built in 1927 and demolished in 1964. Note the grill worked added to the front baggage bin door of the coach, providing cooling ventilation for an electric generator. *Don Coffin collection*

Greyhound Lines President Arthur S. Genet stands at the entry door of GC-13 (PD4501-514). Note the Greyhound drumhead badge mounted on the rear of the coach. *Don Coffin collection*

Anheuser-Busch executives meet their Greyhound provided driver in front of their corporate headquarters in St. Louis, Missouri. *Don Coffin collection*

A small exhaust tailpipe from the generator set stowed in the forward baggage bin compartment on (PD4501-514) can be seen below the rear bumper in this photograph. *Fred Rayman collection*

"The Anheuser" (PD4501-514) appears on this Budweiser advertising matchbook cover. The message reads: "The next time business or pleasure brings you to St. Louis, Newark or Los Angeles Please reserve an hour or two to visit the home of Budweiser." *Fred Rayman collection*

One of several Scenicruisers sent to Korea, #906 was photographed May 28, 1977. *Fred Rayman collection*

Korea Greyhound #913 photographed in Seoul, South Korea, in May of 1973. *Fred Rayman collection*

A road weary Central Greyhound Lines C-1201 (PD4501-370) photographed on May 28, 1962, in Tulsa, Oklahoma. This coach still wore the second "Scenicruiser Service" livery and still had the twin engines installed. *Fred Rayman collection*

"Scenicruiser Service" Western Greyhound Lines P-2311 (PD4501-748) in Los Angeles, California, in January of 1960. *Bryan Cooper collection*

A rear shot of Western Greyhound Lines P-2311 (PD4501-748) in Los Angeles, California, in February of 1960. *Bryan Cooper collection*

Western Greyhound Lines 8160 (PD4501-870) in Los Angeles, California, in 1964. *Bryan Cooper collection*

Western Greyhound Lines 1378 (PD4501-482) in Santa Barbara, California, in January of 1967. *Bryan Cooper collection*

A wonderful example of a classic battery-operated tin toy Scenicruiser produced in Japan. *Fred Rayman collection*

Examples of memorabilia: an original 1954 operating manual for the Scenicruiser, Greyhound Post House Restaurant menu from Washington D.C., a 1963 calendar, 1964 New York World's Fair luggage tag, and an early advertising brochure introducing the Scenicruiser to the traveling public. *Tom McNally collection*

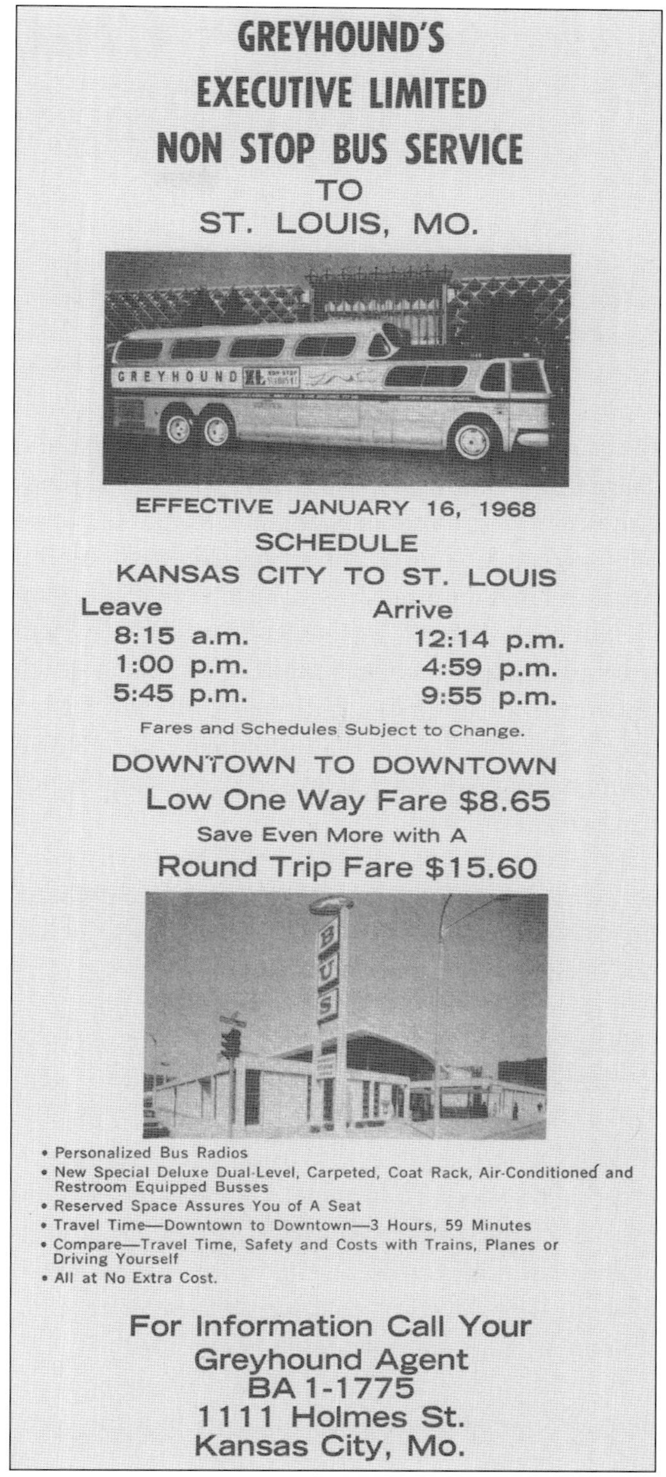

GREYHOUND'S
EXECUTIVE LIMITED
NON STOP BUS SERVICE
TO
ST. LOUIS, MO.

EFFECTIVE JANUARY 16, 1968
SCHEDULE
KANSAS CITY TO ST. LOUIS

Leave	Arrive
8:15 a.m.	12:14 p.m.
1:00 p.m.	4:59 p.m.
5:45 p.m.	9:55 p.m.

Fares and Schedules Subject to Change.

DOWNTOWN TO DOWNTOWN
Low One Way Fare $8.65
Save Even More with A
Round Trip Fare $15.60

- Personalized Bus Radios
- New Special Deluxe Dual-Level, Carpeted, Coat Rack, Air-Conditioned and Restroom Equipped Busses
- Reserved Space Assures You of A Seat
- Travel Time—Downtown to Downtown—3 Hours, 59 Minutes
- Compare—Travel Time, Safety and Costs with Trains, Planes or Driving Yourself
- All at No Extra Cost.

For Information Call Your
Greyhound Agent
BA 1-1775
1111 Holmes St.
Kansas City, Mo.

A rarely seen advertisement for Greyhound Personalized Radio Service appears on the back side of a Kansas City – St. Louis Executive Limited service time table folder, circa 1968. *Fred Rayman collection*

More examples of memorabilia: a children's activity travel playbook produced by Greyhound, large oversized souvenir Post House Restaurant matchbook, and more. *Tom McNally collection*

Chapter 4: Rebuilding the Scenicruiser

The mechanical problems that plagued the original Scenicruiser eventually led to a civil lawsuit. *Time* magazine reported the following on August 6, 1956: "A SUIT AGAINST G.M. is planned by Greyhound, the automaker's best bus customer. Greyhound charges that 570 out of 1,000 double-deck, air-conditioned Scenicruiser buses purchased from G.M. for $53 million developed lubrication troubles." Within two and a half months, *Time* printed the following on October 22, 1956: "G.M.-GREYHOUND FEUD is being patched up out of court. Greyhound gets a settlement for dropping its threat to sue automaker on charge that half the 1,000 double-deck G.M. Scenicruiser buses bought by Greyhound developed mechanical trouble."

By 1957 it became painfully obvious to the management at Greyhound that the twin four-cylinder diesel power plants in the Scenicruisers were an all-but-failure. The fluid coupling arrangement and original electrically controlled clutches were among several mechanical maintenance headaches. Searching for alternative options in the late 1950s, two Scenicruisers (E-5620, PD4501-926 & C-1781, PD4501-872) were test-fitted with a turbo-charged six-cylinder Mack ENDT673 diesel engine and 10-speed manual transmission. On these test coaches, a four-cylinder Continental diesel engine was also mounted in the rear of the coach to drive the air-conditioning system. In addition, Greyhound experimented with Cummins, Mercedes-Benz, and MAN engine combinations, as possible replacements. Upon the eventual development of the eight-cylinder Detroit Diesel in early 1959, it was decided that the 8V-71 would be the replacement engine for the approximate 987 remaining Scenicruisers. A rebuilding program was designed, and Marmon-Herrington of Indianapolis, Indiana, was awarded the $10-million dollar project. GM was offered the contract with Greyhound, but declined due to their already tenuous relationship.

The rebuilding of the Scenicruiser fleet lasted 11 months, starting in October of 1961. Most of the work was completed in Indianapolis, but about $3 million dollars more was spent at various Greyhound garages across the U.S.

In Indianapolis, besides replacing the two 4-71 engines with the single 8V-71, the original three-speed manual transmission was also removed in favor of a non-synchronized Spicer four-speed manual gearbox. An electric solenoid switch was utilized to shift into reverse gear. The quick-change "power-pack" engine cradle method was retained with the new replacement engine mounted straight-in, with the front of the engine facing rear. The exterior of the coach was repainted blue and white and included two gold reflective Scotchlite stripes to celebrate Greyhound's 50th anniversary (in 1964). The new Greyhound lettering used on the outside of the bus was large block style. Interestingly, the updated reflective running dog logo used on the rear of the coach was not the same as that which appeared on the sides. The name "Scenicruiser" along the beltline was changed to "Super Scenicruiser." During the gold-stripe livery years, the 4501 wore five different beltline slogans that all touted the qualities of Going Greyhound. The company replaced the lighted running dog emblem from the nose with an embossed aluminum "puppy plate." A single engine-access door, hinged at the top, replaced a pair of swinging doors that were hinged along the outside. The twin radiators facing rear were deleted, because a new larger single unit was installed at the left side of the engine compartment. Most of the radiator and air-conditioning condenser doors were redesigned to hinge at the front instead of at the top. Most of the aluminum louvers on these doors were replaced by expanded metal mesh panels during the rebuild. The vertical "push bars" that once appeared on the front bumper, as well as the fog lights, were now removed. Some of the split hinged, two-piece opening windows at the entry door and driver's window were changed to solid, non-opening glass. Some of these changes were made at local division shops around the country at varying times. Some of the aluminum rear bumpers were swapped for a chromed steel version. A new air operated parking brake, mounted on the trailing axle, replaced the old-style mechanical system. Safety features such as four-way emergency flashers and side-mounted turn signals were also added.

Western Greyhound Lines 8113 (PD4501-276) in Cedar Rapids, Iowa, on February 4, 1961. *Loring M. Lawrence collection*

Structural issues were addressed during the Marmon-Herrington program as well. Some of the coaches had stress cracks developing along the sides. This was corrected by installing riveted steel gusset plates in several varying locations: between the upper-deck side windows, above the baggage bins, and above the tandem axles. These repairs were performed on an as-needed basis; not all of them received this plating service. Installing repair gusset plates continued to be an on-going maintenance issue that was managed throughout the coach's tenure at Greyhound.

Interior changes were plentiful too. The lower level was repainted in medium metallic green. Floor coverings went from white to green vinyl. The 10 seats on the lower level were reupholstered in the original gold style fabric, but it now included turquoise side panels. With the engine conversion, the appropriate changes were made to the instrument panel. For this rebuild program, the upper-level interior was left untouched. New operators' manuals and maintenance manuals, which outlined all the new features of the 4501R, as it was called, were issued.

An unknown number of Cruisers, maybe around 500, were rebuilt for a second time in about 1970. The exterior was repainted in what is generally described as the red-stripe livery. A darker shade of blue, larger block letters, and a single Red Stripe along the sides were applied. Belt-line slogans, as well as the "Super Scenicruiser" moniker remained. Some of the 4501s wore this paint scheme until the end of their service. Unfortunately, all the three-inch-wide trim moldings and fluted aluminum panels between the windows were removed. The lower interiors were repainted a light yellow (different from that in 1954) with light-yellow side panels, driver's seat, and entry door hinge cover. The upper level paint was changed to light blue at this time. The seats were reupholstered as well. The color of the floor covering was changed back to white. No mechanical change was made at that time.

The four roof-mounted skylights can be seen in this overhead photograph of Southern Greyhound Lines 5542 (PD4501-895). *Don Coffin collection*

This night photo of Southern Greyhound Lines 5542 (PD4501-895) captures the 3M Scotch-Cal reflective lettering and stripes of the Greyhound 50th Anniversary livery. *Don Coffin collection*

The destination sign reads "Chicago Express" on this Gold Stripe livery Southern Greyhound Lines 5552 (PD4501-905). *Don Coffin collection*

Southern Greyhound Lines 5462 (PD4501-355) photographed by Fred Rayman in Oklahoma City, Oklahoma, In August of 1970. *Fred Rayman collection*

Eastern Greyhound Lines 4272 (PD4501-206) at Riverside, California, depot on March 3, 1968. *Fred Rayman collection*

The Riverside, California, depot provided the backdrop for this photo of Eastern Greyhound Lines 4300 (PD4501-056) on May 12, 1968. *Fred Rayman collection*

Western Greyhound Lines 1444 (PD4501-498) gold stripe in New York City in October of 1970. *Jim Husing collection*

Inside cover of an 18-page booklet introducing the Scenicruiser, published by Greyhound Lines in 1954. *Tom McNally collection*

A four-page booklet featuring travel deals that was originally attached to 1965 magazine advertisements. *Tom McNally collection*

A 12-page booklet highlighting the history of Greyhound Lines, published in 1965. *Tom McNally collection*

Souvenir six-page booklet introducing the Scenicruiser in 1954. *Tom McNally collection*

Western Greyhound Lines 8146 (PD4501-725) in San Francisco, California. *Jim Husing collection*

Western Greyhound Lines 9006 in February of 1974. *Jim Husing collection*

Western Greyhound Lines 9052 in September of 1973. *Jim Husing collection*

Western Greyhound Lines 9068 (PD4501-916) in July of 1970. *Jim Husing collection*

Seven gold stripe Scenicruisers line up along 7th Street, near the Greyhound shops in San Francisco, California in May of 1973. *Jim Husing collection*

Western Greyhound Lines 9072 travels a California freeway on April 7, 1973. *Jim Husing collection*

Western Greyhound Lines 9082 (PD4501-462) near the Bayshore Freeway, San Francisco, California, in June of 1970. *Jim Husing collection*

Western Greyhound Lines 9097 (PD4501-565) in California on May 25, 1970. *Jim Husing collection*

This color postcard reads, "Fabens, Texas, 'The Cotton Capitol.'" *Tom McNally collection*

Big Spring, Texas's Greyhound Bus Station and Post House cafeteria with Hotel Settles in background. Big Spring was a major transportation center with schedules to all points. *Tom McNally collection*

Glendale, Nevada was a popular tourist stop on Highway 91 between Las Vegas and St. George, Utah, where the finest foods and overnight accommodations were available. *Tom McNally collection*

Van Horn (in West Texas), at the junction of U.S. 80, U.S. 90 and interstate 10, proclaims this is "Where The West Is." *Tom McNally collection*

Western Greyhound Lines 9098 was, in this photo, parked at Walt's Diner located at 7th Street, and King in San Francisco, California in September of 1970. *Jim Husing collection*

Western Greyhound Lines 8001t (PD4501-738) was one of several 47-passenger commuter buses used on the Travis Air Force Base run located in Fairfield, California. *Jim Husing collection*

Western Greyhound Lines 9664 (PD4501-733) in California on January 22, 1977. *Jim Husing collection*

Western Greyhound Lines 8222 in gold stripe livery was photographed by Fred Rayman in Iowa City, Iowa, in August of 1968. *Fred Rayman collection*

Provo, Utah, provides the beautiful background for Western Greyhound Lines 8261(PD4501-523) in September of 1966. *Fred Rayman collection*

Western Greyhound Lines 1466 (PD4501-735) at the Joplin, Missouri, depot on May 19, 1967. *Fred Rayman collection*

Rear shot of Western Greyhound Lines 8224 at the Lacrosse, Wisconsin, depot on September 19, 1967. *Fred Rayman collection*

"The best things in life don't have to be expensive," according to an ad in *Look* magazine in 1965. *Tom McNally collection*

Western Greyhound Lines 8160 in Cedar Rapids, Iowa, on April 9, 1967. *Fred Rayman collection*

Here's one of several Greyhound Lines advertisements that appeared in the late sixties through the late seventies offering PD-4501 Scenicruisers for sale to the general public. *Tom McNally collection*

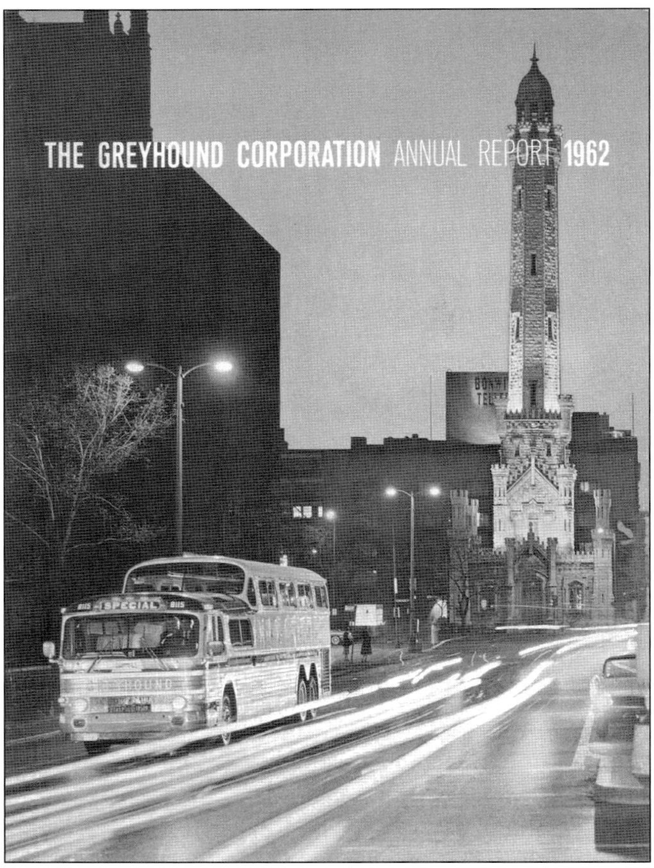

Western Greyhound Lines 8115 (PD4501-314) at dusk along Chicago's Michigan Avenue, facing historic Water Tower Place. This photo was used on the cover of the Greyhound Corporation 1962 annual report. *Fred Rayman collection*

Eastern Greyhound Lines 4276 (PD4501-175) shares the highway with a 1961 Lincoln Continental. *Don Coffin collection*

Eastern Greyhound Lines 4396 (PD4501-584) parked at the Washington D.C. garage on March 20, 1966. *Loring M. Lawrence collection*

Gold stripe Eastern Greyhound Lines 4351 (PD4501-286). *Don Coffin collection*

Central Greyhound Lines 1190 (PD4501-278) emerges from the lower level of the Chicago Greyhound Terminal. Buses entered the passenger loading area (two floors underground) from Lower Wacker Drive. *Bill Luke collection*

Western Greyhound Lines 8100 (PD4501-007) in downtown Minneapolis, Minnesota in April of 1967. *Fred Rayman collection*

Western Greyhound Lines 8174 (PD4501-186) was towed from the snow in St. Paul, Minnesota on March 24, 1966. *Fred Rayman collection*

Western Greyhound Lines 8172 (PD4501-121) at the Lantern Café in downtown Tama, Iowa, on July 8, 1967. *Fred Rayman collection*

Eastern Greyhound Lines 4424 (PD4501-702) in downtown Indianapolis, Indiana, in October of 1966. *Fred Rayman collection*

Southern Greyhound Lines 5458 (PD4501-290) photographed by Fred Rayman in Oklahoma City, Oklahoma in May of 1970. *Fred Rayman collection*

Central Greyhound Lines 1450 (PD4501-546) in downtown St. Louis, Missouri in October of 1966. *Fred Rayman collection*

Greyhound Terminal and Post House Restaurant at Flagstaff, Arizona. *Fred Rayman collection*

Amarillo, Texas, Greyhound Bus Station and Post House in downtown Amarillo. *Tom McNally collection*

Greyhound Bus Terminal, Kansas City, Mo.

Greyhound Bus Terminal on 12th & Holmes, Kansas City, Missouri was a new and beautiful terminal erected at a cost of over 3.5 million dollars to provide excellent services and facilities including restaurant and 900 car parking garage. This building was demolished in 2001 to make way for a parking lot. *Tom McNally collection*

The Post House, on I.H. 90-94 in scenic Wisconsin Dells, is the new Interstate Hi-way Post House. The distinctive red-roofed cafeteria seated 128 persons, serving travelers, vacationers, local residents and Greyhound bus passengers. In addition to excellent food, souvenirs and gifts were also available. The Dells area is noted for scenic boat trips and Indian pageantry. *Tom McNally collection*

Western Greyhound Lines 8183 (PD4501-326) in Provo, Utah, in September of 1966. *Fred Rayman collection*

Southern Greyhound Lines 5406 (PD4501-058) on November 7, 1965, in Key West, Florida. *Fred Rayman collection*

Eastern Greyhound Lines 4425 (PD4501-703) in St. Louis, Missouri, in October of 1966. *Fred Rayman collection*

Western Greyhound Lines 8169 (PD4501-096) in November of 1967, parked inside the Minneapolis, Minnesota Greyhound garage. *Fred Rayman collection*

Western Greyhound Lines 8068 (PD4501-459) appears in the second paint scheme. Note the original two-piece hinged driver's window. *Fred Rayman collection*

Western Greyhound Lines 8125 (PD4501-398) photographed in Halifax, Nova Scotia. Note the vertical "push guards" on the front bumper have already been removed from this particular coach. *Fred Rayman collection*

Western Greyhound Lines 9670 (PD4501-780). This coach was converted to 47 passengers for commuter service. *Roy Hall collection*

The Saturday Evening Post Advertisement: "Travel Refreshed...free from driving strain!" *Tom McNally collection*

Florida Greyhound Lines F-707 (PD4501-069) appears in this *Saturday Evening Post* advertisement. *Tom McNally collection*

Western Greyhound Lines 8203 (PD4501-346) was photographed at a northern Minnesota rest stop, along the Minneapolis-Seattle schedule, by Bill Luke.

Multiple license plates can be seen on the front of Western Greyhound Lines 8212 (PD4501-320) in Oklahoma City, Oklahoma. Prior to "Apportioned License Plates," buses and trucks had to display plates for every state in which they operated. *Fred Rayman collection*

Western Greyhound Lines 8270 (PD4501-606) and 8122 (PD4501-359) at a northern Minnesota rest stop. *Bill Luke collection*

Western Greyhound Lines 8242 (PD4501-486) seen in the background at the 1969 Boy Scouts of America at the National Scout Jamboree held in Farragut, Idaho. Thirty-four thousand people were in attendance for the outdoor event. *Fred Rayman collection*

A selection of Greyhound Scenicruiser memorabilia. *Tom McNally collection*

Souvenir Japanese-made tin toy Scenicruiser models. *Fred Rayman collection*

Two examples of tin Scenicruiser models, and one rarely seen model made of cardboard. *Fred Rayman collection*

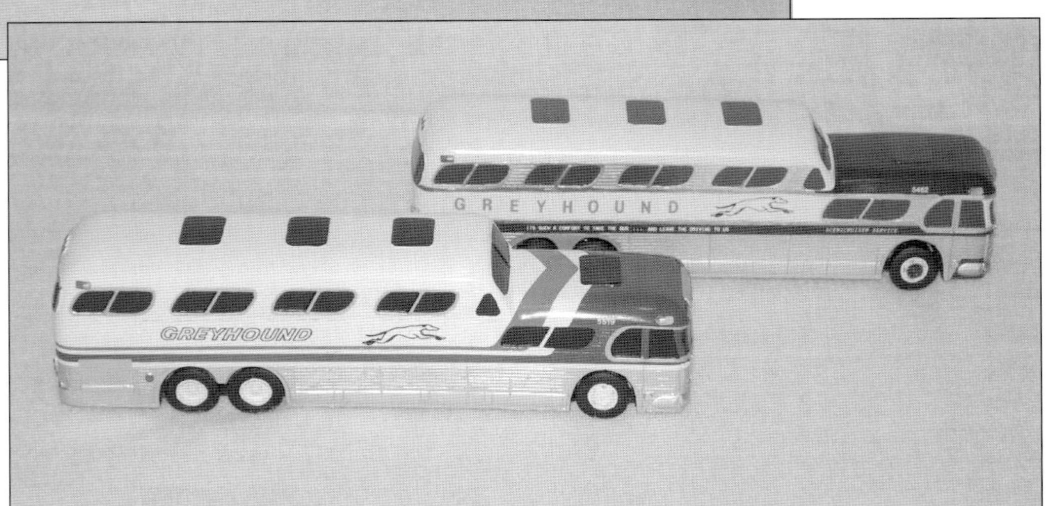

Two 1:48-scale plaster-cast Scenicruiser models produced by Bob Garrett. *Fred Rayman collection*

Factory publicity photo introducing the gold stripe Super Scenicruiser paint scheme for Greyhound's upcoming 1964 50th Anniversary. *Fred Rayman collection*

Western Greyhound Lines 8240 (PD4501-912) shown in San Francisco bound as "Los Angeles Express." *Fred Rayman collection*

The slogan on the beltline of Western Greyhound Lines combo car 0714 (PD4501-238) reads: "Discover America... Go Greyhound... and leave the driving to us." Photographed by Bill Luke in Minneapolis, Minnesota.

This photo of Eastern Greyhound Lines 4276 (PD4501-175) appeared on a Greyhound Scenicruiser timetable schedule on January 3, 1963. *Fred Rayman collection*

Southern Greyhound Lines 5464 (PD4501-357) in Montreal, Canada. *Tom McNally collection*

Eastern Greyhound Lines 4329 (Pd4501-305) in Miami, Florida, circa 1972. *Tom McNally collection*

Southern Greyhound Lines 5443 (PD4501-214) in Richmond, Virginia, on August 27, 1965. *Bruce Korusek collection*

Eastern Greyhound Lines 4362 (PD4501-313) in Boston, Massachusetts, on February 4, 1968. *Bruce Korusek collection*

This 1960 postcard reads: "Martin's Cafeteria – Gila Bend, Arizona Phone 4121 U.S. Highway 80 Delicious Food – Novelties – Curios A must for Southwestern Desert Travelers. Agency Pacific Greyhound Lines." *Tom McNally Collection*

This circa 1956 postcard reads: "Coach House – Niles, Michigan 24 hour Cafeteria Service – Catering to the traveling public." *Tom McNally Collection*

A 1957 postcard reads: "Greyhound Inn Motel – Somerset, Kentucky (South on U.S. Route 27) Greyhound Inn is located in the foothills of the Cumberland Mountains, six miles from Cumberland Lake. The Greyhound Inn offers air-conditioned rooms, 24-hour restaurant service and free transportation to and from scenic Cumberland Lake, and the best fishing location in the state of Kentucky." *Tom McNally Collection*

Central of New York Greyhound Lines C-1085 (PD4501-043) appears on this "Greetings from Pecos, Texas" postcard. *Tom McNally Collection*

Western Greyhound Lines 8035 (PD4501-833) in downtown Kansas City, Missouri, on May 8, 1967. *Fred Rayman collection*

Eastern Greyhound Lines 4428 (PD4501-709) at the Dubuque, Iowa, terminal on July 20, 1966. *Fred Rayman collection*

Eastern Greyhound Lines 4258 (PD4501-101) in St. Louis, Missouri, in October of 1966. *Fred Rayman collection*

Eastern Greyhound Lines 4229 (PD4501-031) in Duluth, Minnesota, on July 10, 1968. *Fred Rayman collection*

Western Greyhound Lines 8063 (PD4501-415) in Minneapolis, Minnesota, on September 24, 1967. *Fred Rayman collection*

Western Greyhound Lines 8050 (PD4501-953) in Cedar Rapids, Iowa, in May of 1967. *Fred Rayman collection*

Central Greyhound Lines 1241 (PD4501-902) in El Paso, Texas in November of 1967. This coach has a non-standard engine access door with deleted louvers. *Fred Rayman collection*

Central Southwestern Greyhound Lines C-1254 (PD4501-023). *Fred Rayman collection*

The new Greyhound Bus depot on 7th between W. Wisconsin and W. Michigan Avenues in Milwaukee, Wisconsin. *Tom McNally collection*

This postcard proclaims: "Waterman's Cafeteria – Rolla, Missouri – Mr. and Mrs. Andy Waterman, owners, agent for Greyhound and M.K. & O Bus Lines. Will seat 200 people. We welcome Charter Buses. Can seat and feed 4 bus loads in 45 minutes. Open 24 hours daily. Driver may call collect – Code 314 – 364-2348." *Tom McNally collection*

This postcard states: "Mueller's Dineateria Van Horn, Texas – Your best stop on U.S. 80 – 90, Texas 54." *Tom McNally collection*

Caption on the rear of this vintage postcard reads: "Greyhound Bus Depot 105 – 3rd Ave. 783-4651 Yuma, Arizona Harry and Oleta Erickson – Agents." *Tom McNally collection*

Central Greyhound Lines 1333 (PD4501-431) traveling through Homestead, Iowa, as the "Chicago Express" in August of 1968. *Fred Rayman collection*

Central Greyhound Lines 1466 (PD4501-735) captured at the Joplin, Missouri, bus depot in June of 1967. *Fred Rayman collection*

Eastern Greyhound Lines 4247 (PD4501-025) wears the second version of the gold stripe paint scheme in Houston, Texas, on July 4, 1971. Note the upper reflective stripe is mounted below the 3-inch molding. *Fred Rayman collection*

The destination sign on Eastern Greyhound Lines 4277 (PD4501-176) reads "New York" while photographed in Chicago, Illinois. Note the original two-piece opening driver's window survives on this coach. *Fred Rayman collection*

Eastern Greyhound Lines 4362 (PD4501-313) shown prior to being involved in a deadly head-on collision with a tractor-trailer truck. The accident, which occurred May 14, 1972 on U.S. 11 West, near Bean Station, Tennessee, claimed the lives of 14 passengers and the driver Frank Flick of Roanoke, Virginia. *Fred Rayman collection*

Central Greyhound Lines 1259 (PD4501-167) photographed at the Oklahoma Transportation Company's garage in Oklahoma City, Oklahoma, on May 11, 1970. *Fred Rayman collection*

This ad proclaimed: "It costs less to take the bus... and leave the driving to us!" Central Greyhound Lines 1454 (PD4501-643), shown here in June of 1962 at Columbia, Missouri, Greyhound Post House was headed to Kansas City, Missouri. *Fred Rayman collection*

Central Greyhound Lines 1455 (PD4501-644) at the St. Louis, Missouri, Greyhound garage. Note the early porcelain enamel Greyhound Lines signs along the top of the building. *Fred Rayman collection*

Eastern Greyhound Lines 4322 (PD4501-665) under tow behind a White brand truck, on the shoulder of Eastbound HWY 401, 1-3/4 miles west of HWY 10 interchange, at Cooksville, Ontario, on July 29, 1967. *Photo by Jack D. Knowles; Loring M. Lawrence collection*

Southern Greyhound Lines 5528 (PD4501-821) at Fort Eustis, Virginia, on December 3, 1966. This coach wears the seldom seen "It costs less" beltline slogan. *Loring M. Lawrence collection*

Central Greyhound Lines 1181 (PD4501-254) at the Oklahoma Transportation Company Garage in Oklahoma City, Oklahoma, on September 30, 1972. *Fred Rayman collection*

Southern Greyhound Lines 5399 (PD4501-1001) in Portland, Maine, circa 1970. Note the absence of the driver's spotlight and left side emergency door that (EXP-331 – PD4501-1001) once had. It is believed that these two non-standard equipment items were removed during the 1961/1962 Marmon-Herrington rebuild. *Loring M. Lawrence collection*

Southern Greyhound Lines 5300 (PD4501-107) in Burlington, Vermont, on October 20, 1964. *Fred Rayman collection*

Southern Greyhound Lines 5421 (PD4501-134) parked at the Greyhound Post House terminal Restaurant in Miami, Florida, on April 17, 1965. *Fred Rayman collection*

Southern Greyhound Lines 5462 (PD4501-355) at Oklahoma Transportation Company garage in Oklahoma City, Oklahoma, in August of 1970. OTC was contracted by Greyhound to perform maintenance and repairs on their fleet, as Greyhound did not have garage facilities in Oklahoma City. *Fred Rayman collection*

Southern Greyhound Lines 5495 (PD4501-633) in Key West, Florida, in May of 1965. *Fred Rayman collection*

Western Greyhound Lines 8100 (PD4501-007) wears its removable winter cover over the engine access door louvers in Cedar Rapids, Iowa, in May of 1967. *Fred Rayman collection*

Western Greyhound Lines 8100 (PD4501-007) parked in downtown Minneapolis, Minnesota, in April of 1967. *Fred Rayman collection*

New York City bound Western Greyhound Lines 8112 (PD4591-275) leaves Provo, Utah, in September of 1966. *Fred Rayman collection*

Western Greyhound Lines 8168 (PD4501-095) bound for San Francisco and photographed in Salt Lake City, Utah, in September of 1966. *Fred Rayman collection*

This 1956 postcard stated: "Greyhound Lines, Travel Host To The Nation, places economical, convenient transportation at your service to all points of interest throughout the United States, Canada, and Mexico." *Tom McNally Collection*

Postmarked 1958, this card read: "Greyhound Post House – Effingham, Illinois. 'The Heart of the Nation.'" *Tom McNally Collection*

This one reads: "Reg & Andy's Café Cafeteria Greyhound Bus Depot, Rolla, Mo. Banquet Room will seat 140 people. Known from coast to coast for our famous ham. Open 24 hours daily. Mr. and Mrs. Reg Waters, owners. Andy Waterman, Mgr." *Tom McNally Collection*

Western Greyhound Lines 8168 (PD4501-095) in Salt Lake City, Utah, in September of 1966. *Fred Rayman collection*

Western Greyhound Lines 8183 (PD4501-326) in Provo, Utah, in September of 1966. *Fred Rayman collection*

Western Greyhound Lines 8126 (PD4501-399) leaves the Minneapolis, Minnesota, terminal for Seattle, Washington, in July of 1966. *Fred Rayman collection*

Western Greyhound Lines 8273 (PD4501-609) leaves Marshalltown, Iowa, in September of 1971. *Fred Rayman collection*

Note the non-standard gold stripe arrangement seen here on Central Greyhound Lines 1160 (PD4501-081) in Colorado Springs, Colorado, in July of 1970. *Fred Rayman collection*

W.G. "Red" Vickers poses in front of a Gold stripe Scenicruiser at the St. Petersburg, Florida, Greyhound Garage circa 1964. *John Vickers collection*

Western Greyhound Lines 8135 (PD4501-456) appears in this June 1965 *Look* magazine advertisement. Note the decal on the passenger entry door promoting the New York World's Fair 1965, and the variety of pre-apportioned system license plates displayed. *Tom McNally collection*

Chapter 5:
Greyhound's XL Service

In 1967, five Scenicruisers were rebuilt and assigned to Greyhound's new Executive Limited non-stop bus service. Three of these special buses ran daily round-trip service from downtown St. Louis, Missouri, to downtown Kansas City, Missouri. The other two dedicated Scenicruisers ran daily round-trip schedules from Houston, Texas, to San Antonio, Texas. When passengers chose these 3-1/2- to 4-hour rides, they could do so with a reserved seat each way. The rarely seen "Personalized Radio Service" was standard on all five of these XL coaches, as were red-carpeted aisle floors and coat racks on the lower level. The exterior of the XL coaches wore a special exclusive paint scheme. The Kansas City/St. Louis service used the following coach serial numbers: PD4501-213, PD4501-214, and PD4501-219. These three buses were even equipped with whitewall tires. Serial numbers PD4501-044 and PD4501-083 were utilized for the Houston/San Antonio runs. XL Service never expanded beyond these four cities. It is believed that this special service ended sometime around 1971.

Wall Street Executive Coach

On March 29, 1971, Greyhound inaugurated its Executive Coach Service, operating one round-trip per day, five days a week, between Hartford, Connecticut, and New York's Wall Street. This special Scenicruiser was available exclusively to passengers from Aetna, Travelers, and The Hartford insurance companies. With "Executive Coach" on the destination sign, PD4501-151 offered a distinctive level of luxury for its passengers. The upper level was furnished with not only standard high-back seats in pairs but also revolving individual lounge chairs. The coach was equipped with curtains, high-intensity reading lights, wall-to-wall carpet, and tables with drink holders. Other changes included the removal of the overhead parcel racks throughout, and the removal of the sunken aisle in the upper level, to create more headroom. The lower level housed the restroom, wardrobe, and a galley that had running water, a hot liquid dispenser, and an ice chest. Eastern Greyhound Lines 4241 wore the brand new red, white, and blue exterior "Red Stripe paint scheme." Custom Coach of Columbus, Ohio, converted the interior of this specially prepared coach. The crew included a dedicated Greyhound driver and two hostesses with alternate schedules every other week. Under the conditions of the agreement with the insurance companies, the bus was never used for weekend charter trips. The only exception to this arrangement was a once-a-year charter of Shell Oil executives to the Army-Navy football game. When the twelve-month contract expired between Greyhound and the insurance companies, PD4501-151 was replaced by a newer MC-7.

Combo cars

Starting in 1967, about 100 Scenicruisers were converted to passenger-freight combination (combo car) coaches. In the days before UPS and FedEx, Greyhound delivered newspapers and all sorts of packages. A combo car had a freight door installed at the right rear by which packages could be loaded and unloaded. A varying number of seats were removed, and a partition was constructed to separate passengers from freight on the upper level. Sometimes the entire upper deck was used to haul freight with all the upper seats removed. The first two coaches reworked for Package Express-combo service were Central Greyhound Lines 1392 (PD4501-601) which was a 22-passenger version and Southern Greyhound Lines 5413 (PD4501-124) which was a 10-passenger version where the entire upper deck was a package express compartment. These coaches were detailed in a Greyhound inter-Office memo, dated December 12, 1967. PD4501-601 became 0799, and PD4501-124 became 0945. 0600 and 0700 series fleet numbers were assigned to Western and Central Greyhound divisions. 0800 and 0900 series fleet numbers were assigned to Eastern and Southern Greyhound divisions. For dispatching purposes, the first "0" digit indicated combo bus, the second digit indicated Greyhound division assignment, and the last two digits were the actual coach's assigned fleet number. When this service began, the first buses carried the gold-stripe livery, then the red-stripe livery, and finally others; introduced in about 1973 was the new red-white-blue "Pepsi" exterior paint scheme.

In the mid 1970s, about 100 Scenics had another row of seats added to the upper level, increasing their capacity from 43 to 47. These new, more crowded buses were pressed into service as commuter shuttles. These buses ran schedules for Travis Air Force Base, San Francisco airport, as well as the San Diego area, and some East Coast commuter hubs also. Most of these commuters remained in their 1962 gold-stripe paint scheme until they were retired. Essentially all the Scenicruisers were either out of service or had been sold off by 1978. By the time the Scenicruisers were sold, they had set records for both continuous years in service and accumulated revenue miles.

XL service, Houston to San Antonio. *Fred Rayman collection*

XL service, St. Louis to Kansas City. *Fred Rayman collection*

Note the whitewall tires on this Scenicruiser showcased on this Timetable schedule for Kansas City – St. Louis Executive Limited service effective January 16, 1968. *Fred Rayman collection*

A seldom seen Scenicruiser Underpass Clearance Manual and a Sonar Guided toy are just a few items in this group of collectibles. *Tom McNally collection*

Coach Builders plate removed from PD4501-482. All the Scenicruisers were equipped with an I.D. plate like this, mounted on the dash, just inside the passenger entry door. *Tom McNally collection*

A wide variety of Japanese tin Scenicruiser model toys. *Fred Rayman collection*

Eastern Greyhound Lines 4241 (PD4501-151) was used as the Executive coach for three insurance companies. This photo was taken in Hartford, Connecticut, where the bus was based. *Jon Hobein collection*

Eastern Greyhound Lines 4241 (PD4501-151) was the Hartford Executive coach, but was owned later by Glenpool High School in Glenpool, Oklahoma; shown here on December 28, 1995. *Fred Rayman collection*

Club Café was an iconic roadside Greyhound Lines stop along U.S. Route 66 in Santa Rosa, New Mexico. *Tom McNally collection*

The Scotch-cal reflective stripes really show up well in this chrome postcard. *Tom McNally collection*

This postcard proclaimed: "America's Favorite Bus: The Super Scenicruiser Greyhound presents the Super Scenicruiser—62 ways better-than-ever. This 43 passenger, gold striped bus features air conditioning, panoramic windows, a complete restroom and air suspension ride. It's such a pleasure to ride this…and leave the driving to us!" *Tom McNally collection*

Central Greyhound Lines 1265 (PD4501-092) at the Santa Rosa, New Mexico, depot. *Fred Rayman collection*

Central Greyhound Lines 1333 (PD4501-431) in Oklahoma City, Oklahoma in January of 1971. This was the very first Scenicruiser to be painted in the Red Stripe paint scheme. *Fred Rayman collection*

After driving a charter run from Oklahoma City to Amarillo, Texas, for Oklahoma Transportation Company, Fred Rayman rode Central Greyhound Lines 1275 (PD4501-237) "cushioned" to return back to Oklahoma City. Fred took this photo at a stop in Shamrock, Texas, in the early June afternoon of 1970. Note the PD-4106 headlights, turn signals, cowl, and front running dog emblem conversion done to this Red Stripe Scenicruiser. *Fred Rayman collection*

The same Central Greyhound Lines 1275 (PD4501-237) later the same day at a stop in Clinton, Oklahoma. Note this coach also had been modified with MCI MC-7 taillights. *Fred Rayman collection*

Passengers board Southern Greyhound 5479 (PD4501-532) in St. Augustine, Florida, in April of 1972. *Fred Rayman collection*

Western Greyhound Lines 8017t (PD4501-754) in San Farncisco, California, on October 18, 1973. Note this coach has the replacement stainless steel front bumper with no holes for the former fog lights. *Jim Husing collection*

Central Greyhound Lines 1459 (PD4501-728) and 1397 (PD4501-656) exploring California in 1972. *Jim Husing collection*

Red Stripe livery Southern Greyhound Lines 5425 (PD4501-140) in Norfolk, Virginia. *Bruce Korusek collection*

Western Greyhound Lines combo car 0621 (PD4501-282). *Bryan Cooper collection*

A vintage Greyhound drivers cap bears a badge that reads: "Greyhound – leave the driving to us – over a million miles a day." A diecast Tootsie toy model, die-cut luggage tag, and humorous postcard, as well as a tin toy and matchbook cover complete this group of memorabilia. *Tom McNally collection*

Western Greyhound Lines combo car 0713 (PD4501-315) after a right-rear tag axle tire fire. *Bryan Cooper collection*

Eastern Greyhound Lines 4371 (PD4501-338). *Bryan Cooper collection*

The gold stripe livery versions were the first Scenicruisers to be converted to Combo Cars. Western Greyhound Lines 0710 (PD4501-233) in Oklahoma City, Oklahoma, in June of 1970. *Fred Rayman collection*

Red Stripe combo car Western Greyhound Lines 0652 (PD4501-524) in September of 1973. *Jim Husing collection*

Western Greyhound Lines 0718 (PD4501-750) "Pepsi-Cola" livery Combo Car In November of 1974. *Jim Husing collection*

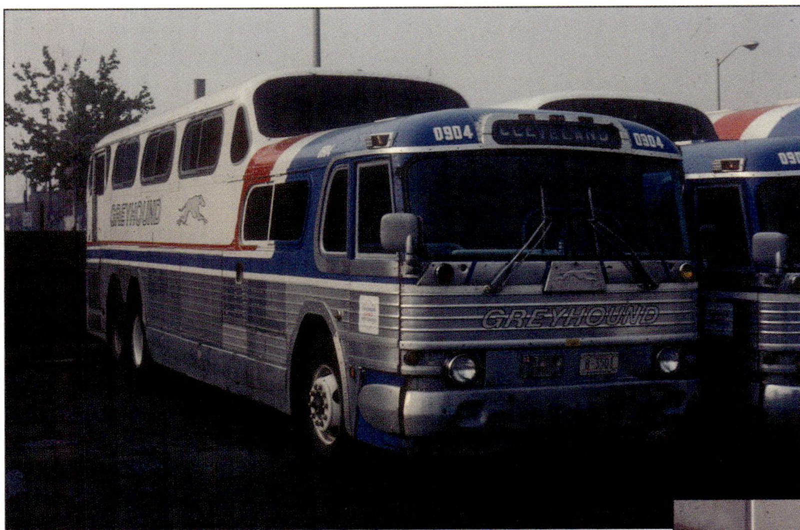

Greyhound Lines Combo Car 0904 (PD4501-058) in Columbus, Ohio, on August 24, 1976. *Bruce Korusek photo; Fred Rayman collection*

Western Greyhound Lines 0645 (PD4501-718) Combo Car. in October of 1973. *Bruce Korusek collection*

Western Greyhound Lines Freight Combo Car 0615 (PD4501-762) in Los Angeles, California, in October of 1977. *Bruce Korusek collection*

Western Greyhound Lines Combo Car 0605 (PD4501-444) in San Francisco, California, in July of 1976. *Fred Rayman collection*

The freight door by which packages were loaded can be easily seen on Western Greyhound Lines 0612 (PD4501-121) in Oklahoma City, Oklahoma, in July of 1976. *Fred Rayman collection*

Western Greyhound Lines Combo Car 0718 (PD4501-750) shown in the "Pepsi-Cola" paint scheme at the Chicago, Illinois, planetarium near Lake Michigan on November 17, 1974. *Fred Rayman collection*

A 26-passenger capacity Combo Freight Car, Western Greyhound Lines 0795 (PD4501-653) departs Beaumont, Texas, bound for Houston, Texas, on April 20, 1975. *Fred Rayman collection*

Western Greyhound Lines 0711 (PD4501-235) in Houston, Texas, in June of 1972. *Fred Rayman collection*

The cargo door and ladder were used to unload freight from this Western Greyhound Lines 0714 (PD4501-238). Note the control button for the roll-up style freight door is mounted to the left of the door opening. There were several varying styles of freight doors used on Combo Cars throughout the years. *Bill Luke collection*

The center rear window on this Combo Car was made of white fiberglass on this Western Greyhound Lines 0626 (PD4501-267) in Oklahoma City, Oklahoma, in May of 1972. *Fred Rayman collection*

Western Greyhound Lines Combo Car 0703 (PD4501-407) in Dallas, Texas, in July of 1973. Note during the 1970 Red Stripe rebuild effort, the fluted trim between the side windows and 3-inch wide beltline trim moldings were removed. Chrome steel replacement rear bumpers were installed on several Scenicruisers like the one shown here. *Fred Rayman collection*

Western Greyhound Lines 0608 (PD4501-391) Red Stripe Combo Car. *Jim Husing collection*

Western Greyhound Lines 0630 (PD4501-064) Combo Car on August 25, 1973. *Jim Husing collection*

A clever 1955 comic postcard featuring a Greyhound Scenicruiser (Holland Tunnel). *Tom McNally collection*

"Low-Cost Luxury Travel" Mount Baker Ski Area (Washington) wall calendar. *Tom McNally collection*

Chapter 6:
Through the Eyes of Others

It's helpful and useful to share some of the experiences of some of the people who, while the Scenicruisers were new, saw them, drove them, maintained them, rode them, and loved them.

Don Coffin is a long-time motor-coach enthusiast. His love of Greyhound buses started about 1934, when he was just 10 years old. He often rode the bus from his boyhood home in Montclair, New Jersey, to his grandfather's dairy farm in Dudley, Massachusetts. Around 1950, while working for the telephone company in New York City, Don saw a newspaper advertisement for an upcoming display of Greyhound's brand-new GX-2 Scenicruiser bus. So, over his lunch break, Don traveled 10 miles to the Newark, New Jersey, Greyhound terminal to have a look at this fantastic new bus. As it happened, Don had befriended a neighbor who was the superintendent of the Capitol Greyhound terminal in New York City. When the GX-2 was displayed in New York City, that neighbor asked Mr. Coffin if he wanted to ride the concept coach from the Pennsylvania Greyhound garage on West 45th Street to the Capitol Greyhound terminal on West 50th Street. The gracious offer was accepted, and Don rode the three or four miles alone on the lower level so he could watch the driver as he operated this mysterious new wonder-of-a-bus. Mr. Coffin is presently 87 years old, and he says he can still visualize the September of 1954 departure of the very first production Scenicruiser to be dispatched from New York City to Miami, Florida. This time it was PD4501-001 (fleet number P-5446) on display at the Capitol Greyhound terminal for about two weeks prior to its maiden voyage. The coach left New York with two drivers and at least one GM engineer on board, bound as a Miami Limited. Don Coffin stood in the terminal driveway and watched it pull away.

John Adams, a retired Greyhound coach operator, shares some of his tales:

"My first trip behind the wheel of a Scenicruiser was on a deadhead assignment from Springfield, Missouri, to Dallas, delivering a new bus to the Dallas shop to be readied for service. The road south of Big Cabin over US-69 was new to me, but I had a ball while driving that new bus with paper still on the floor and the smell of 'new' all over. In the Oklahoma hills south of Atoka everything was going right. On the upgrade with the gearshift lever in high and the two-speed button on low for power, I was catching trucks and cars at the top with my speed up and the road clear ahead. With a flip of the button back to high-high, I was off and running, with the slower traffic falling behind. At Durant, Oklahoma, I saw the semaphore marking the Greyhound station, and I pulled over to bump my tires. While I was walking around the rear of the bus, an automobile came sliding to a stop alongside the bus in a cloud of dust. As the driver walked up to me, he asked, 'Is this the bus to Dallas?' I told him that I was taking a new bus to Dallas, and I asked if he was looking for the scheduled bus. He said, 'Yeah. I was waiting in Atoka to put my mother-in-law on the Dallas bus when I saw you go through, and I thought we had missed it.' I told him that if he would wait at Durant, the scheduled bus would be through. I then asked about the roads on to Dallas, and I asked if he thought I could make Dallas by dark. He said: 'If that son of a bitch will run over those wide Texas roads like it ran over that cow trail back there, you won't have any trouble.'

"The two windshields (upper and lower) led to a new bus driver joke: Two crows nesting west of Springfield, Missouri, near Halltown missed no chance to fly over the windshield of oncoming buses and drop their loads. They sat on a telephone line one day as a new Scenicruiser approached, and one crow said to the other, 'Shall we?' The second crow replied, 'Sure. Why not?' They flew up into the air and began their bombing run, unaware that they were diving on a new bus with two windshields. As they cleared the first windshield with bombs away, the upper deck windshield caught them and knocked them senseless into the ditch. When they finally revived and began stumbling around trying to knock the dust off their feathers, one crow said to the other, 'Damn! Did you ever see a second section following so close?'

"Drivers eventually found that the Scenicruiser had a 'seventh' gear. By easing the gearshift lever forward while running in high-high, you could touch the switch that stepped up the rpm's as though you had flipped the button to low-high—but you were still in high-high with increased RPM's, stepping the speed up to 80 or 85 mph. This seventh gear was discovered by accident, probably by some driver running along in high-high with his hand resting on the gearshift knob while the vibration of the bus gradually eased the shift lever forward. I can imagine his surprise when his bus suddenly leaped forward; moving up to around 85 mph from the 65 mph governed speed. Word of this seventh gear spread across the U.S. like wildfire and the company put out bulletins making it a firing offense to use the seventh gear.

"I'm sure all of us used the seventh gear at times, perhaps with some guilt or trepidation. I remember slipping into seventh gear east of Carthage, Missouri, en route to Springfield on a long straight stretch of Route 66. I was running late, trying to make up time, and I promised myself that I would never do it again. I probably did do it again—a few times.

"In the mid 1960s, while I drove out of Kansas City, I was asked to come off the road long enough to cover dispatchers' vacations in the dispatch office. This seldom lasted more than a month or two, but invariably I began kicking my butt after the first few days for having agreed to come off the road. I remember leaving Kansas City one sunny morning on a charter to Garden City, Kansas, after working in the dispatch office. The sun lay in my lap, and the front end of the Scenicruiser gently rocked up and down as we cruised down the highway, and I said to myself, 'Why would anyone ever want to do anything else?'"

Ron Van Kleeck remembers joining Southern Greyhound Lines in Miami, Florida, as a mechanic in 1961. He had initially wanted to hire on as a driver, but he was told that, at 31 years old, he had exceeded the maximum age of 30 to become a Greyhound driver. It was explained that, if a person had previous non-Greyhound company driving experience, that was considered a liability in their opinion, as one may have developed bad driving habits. So Ron went to work in the garage and soon the body shop, where he overhauled coaches, including Scenicruisers. Removing seats, windows, and all interior components was just part of what was done in the Miami shops. The Scenics he was repairing had apparently already been through Marmon-Herrington, and had the single-engine conversions completed. Structural side plates installation, bulkhead replacement, and minor accident repairs were all part of Ron's efforts. He describes using a template and jigsaw to cut the mounting holes in overhead parcel racks to install the personalized AM radios. Van-Kleeck comments, "Changing the alternator through that little access hole in the rear aisle was the worst repair to do on the coach." He continues, "Some guys would get frustrated and remove the entire engine with a forklift, because it would allow better access, and was quicker." The Southern Greyhound division was very strict with the performance of their mechanics and the appearance of their buses, according to Ron VanKleeck. They even demanded that all the mechanics' toolboxes were painted the same color. Detroit Diesel green and yellow were both considered before they settled on bright red. Ron enjoyed working on the Scenics, and he always looked forward to test-driving them before they were put back into scheduled service.

When W. G. "Red" Vickers began his driving career at Florida Motor Lines in 1934, he drove Jacksonville to Miami round-trips. That company's name was eventually changed to Florida Greyhound lines when Greyhound bought them out in 1946. Red's son, John Vickers, remembers his family moving to Pinellas Park, Florida, in 1950. It was at this time when young John started riding from St. Petersburg to Tallahassee on his dad's Greyhound schedule whenever he could. He remembers these early trips with his dad were aboard GMC PD-3751 Silversides. This soon changed when Florida Greyhound Lines received their first Scenicruiser in 1954. John was just 12 years old when his dad took him to the Greyhound Depot on Central Avenue in downtown St. Petersburg for a display of PD4501-002 (fleet number F-701). It was love at first sight, and Vickers has been a Scenicruiser fan ever since. When he was old enough, John dropped his father off at work on weekends, so he could use the family's 1950 Chevrolet. John often helped his dad with pre-trip inspections of lights, tires, oil, and coolant, and most importantly, checking the fuel card to verify the bus had been properly fueled. The Greyhound maintenance shop was close to the depot, so he rode along with his dad over to the station. After the passengers were loaded, the father and son told each other good-bye. Most of the Tallahassee trips, John remembers, were aboard Scenicruiser equipment on through service to Chicago, Illinois.

John served in the U.S. Air Force, stationed at Amarillo AFB, Texas, from 1962 to 1966. From the break-room window on the base, he watched for the eastbound Greyhound Scenicruiser New York Express every morning. He could look just beyond the flight line at old Route 66 and see the gold-stripe Scenic pass through Amarillo almost always right on schedule.

D.B. "Doc" Rushing grew up at Greyhound (1940-1961) in Nashville, Tennessee, while his father drove for Greyhound (1940-1977), starting with the Southeastern Greyhound Lines. Doc says that he became hooked on the coaches and everything about them as a young child—literally longer ago than he can recall. He started riding with his father at age 3, first between the shop and the station, then on same-day round-trips, later on overnight trips with layovers. He delighted in riding the ACF and ACF-Brill coaches, then the Silversides, the 4103, the 4104, and eventually the "fantabulous" Scenicruiser. He intently watched every movement his father made while driving, and he fantasized about driving a Dog himself, especially aboard the unmatched Scenicruiser. He regards the Cruiser as his favorite coach and the King of the Road. Eventually Doc achieved an old childhood dream; for three years he too drove for Greyhound, between two of his other careers.

Stephen "Skip" Malone rode many Scenicruisers between his home in Birmingham, Alabama, and Athens, Alabama, where he attended Athens College. From January of 1966 through December of 1969, Skip became friendly with the Greyhound drivers and loved sitting within the first two or three rows upstairs and seeing out the front upper windshields. He became fascinated with riding aboard the Scenic, and he claims they were always a delight to ride. After graduating from college in 1970, he rode his favorite bus one last time aboard a combo car, in the spring of 1975.

Chapter 7: Life After Greyhound

It has been said that Greyhound initially did not want to sell the remaining Scenicruisers to anyone, because the coaches were so integral to the identity of the company. In the end, about 400 Cruisers entered the used-bus market. For many private charter-bus companies, schools, churches, and bands, the retirement of the Scenicruisers from the Greyhound fleet in the late 1960s and early 1970s was the first opportunity to own a 40-foot dual-level bus. The first 4501 painted in non-Greyhound livery was that of X-64, which belonged to California Parlor Cars, a subsidiary of Greyhound. The first Scenicruiser to be sold off from Greyhound went to a company that specialized in the resale of used bus equipment, Hausman bus sales in Chicago, Illinois. A salesman from Hausman placed a call to Spike Michaud, of Michaud Bus Lines, located in Salem, Massachusetts. Michaud immediately leaped at the opportunity to acquire the coach (PD4501-591). A few days later the bus was picked up in Chicago, in October of 1968, and began charter service for Michaud as number 181. Approximately two months later Michaud bought a second cruiser (PD4501-800) through Hausman, and it was retrieved directly from the Greyhound Depot in Montgomery, Alabama. Incidentally, years earlier, S/N 800 had been Greyhound Gold Stripe livery-fleet #5522, and was used for plaster models that were displayed at Greyhound Depots. Added improvements, such as whitewall tires and chrome hubcaps, helped distinguish Michaud's touring coaches. In an attempt to modernize their first 4501, they added the four-headlight system from the newer PD4106.

Dave Millhouser and John Oakman began working as mechanics and bus drivers for a non-profit Christian organization known as Young Life in the summer of 1969. In the early 1970s, Young Life began a national bus program designed to transport high-school children to summer camps. The fleet, which included about a dozen Scenicruisers, was based in Buena Vista, Colorado. Millhouser describes the Scenics he once drove as "having a good turning radius, sufficient handling, and were great to drive once you mastered the shift linkage." John Oakman also has pleasant memories of the Scenicruisers, and claims his early experiences have enabled him to establish a long and successful career in the motorcoach industry. According to Oakman, they became proficient at removing the coach engines for repairs in as little as 45 minutes. Oakman adds, "They were very dependable. We would put 50,000 miles on them each summer. They would run and run." After their experiences together at Young Life, Millhouser and Oakman remained lifelong friends.

The Cruiser became a thing of legend among musicians and touring bands. Arlo Guthrie, Hoyt Axton, and James Brown were among a few faithful followers of this coach. Scores of colleges, high schools, drum and bugle corps, and churches all traveled on their very own Scenicruisers. The Reverend Billy Graham acquired Central Greyhound Lines 1176 (PD4501-242), and had it shipped to Africa for use in his Evangelistic Crusades. Even Greyhound's competitors, including Central Texas Trailways, of Waco, Texas, acquired several retired Scenicruisers for their fleet.

Michaud Bus Lines of Salem, Massachusetts, bought the first Scenicruiser (PD4501-591) to be sold away from Greyhound Lines in October of 1968. The coach was now called "Yankee Traveler" and was designated Michaud #181. *Jim Michaud collection*

"The Action Trav'lers," a non-profit group specializing in educational youth trips to Mexico, was founded by Robert Winter III of Valdosta, Georgia. They took their first "Mexitour" camping trip aboard a converted school bus in 1968. As the group grew in size, they would eventually graduate to a small fleet of two GMC PD-4104s, and one PD-4501 Scenicruiser. *Robert Winter III collection*

This photo shows the Teotihuacan, Archaeological site in Mexico. Eastern Greyhound Lines (PD4501-766) was sold to the Sabres Edge Drum and Bugle Corps of Missouri. The coach broke-down in Valdosta, Georgia, and the Action Trav'lers then bought it on the courthouse steps for what was owed on a mechanic's lien. In addition, $10,000 was raised from the sale of Solar Viewers for the 1971 Total Solar Eclipse in South Georgia that year. It was enough to buy a second coach (PD4104-3568), which they named "Solar Express" for The Action Trav'lers! *Robert Winter III collection*

Members of "The Action Trav'lers" prepare PD4501-766 for a trip to Mexico. They were now an official GM Dealer and kept new and donated parts on hand for their coaches. The children were taught to rebuild clutches, engines, transmissions, and electrical systems for their fleet. *Robert Winter III collection*

1970s R&B music sensations "Kool and The Gang" toured on their very own Scenicruiser. Here is their PD4501-479 at the Oklahoma Transportation Company garages in Oklahoma City, Oklahoma, in July of 1973. *Fred Rayman collection*

The Chi-Lites were a band formed in Chicago in 1959. The smooth soul vocal quartet made it big in the 1970s with several hit records. Their coach seen here was photographed in Houston, Texas, in December of 1972. *Fred Rayman collection*

The Boy Scouts of America on a charter with Vancouver-Portland Bus Company In August of 1973. *Bill Luke photo; Fred Rayman collection*

PD4501-687 belonged to the Christian youth group "Young Life" shown here in Colorado Springs, Colorado, in August of 1974. *Fred Rayman collection*

PD4501-094 was owned by Amarillo Christian Schools and was photographed at a "Bus Bash" convention on September 11, 1994, in Amarillo, Texas. *Fred Rayman collection*

Golden Isle Coaches of Jacksonville, Florida, owned PD4501-005, seen here in Winter Garden, Florida, in June of 1984. *Fred Rayman collection*

PD4501-074 was bought directly from Greyhound for use as a high school sports and band transport coach by the "Fighting Tigers" of Ironton, Ohio. In service at the school for more than twenty years, it was lovingly maintained by the Lawless family, a father and son team who were mechanics and automotive shop teachers. The bus was photographed by Ron Van Kleech at Disney World, Orlando, Florida, on December 26, 1993. *Fred Rayman collection*

PD4501-104 was used for promotion of "Billy Rays BBQ" restaurant located in Tulsa, Oklahoma, in February of 1997. *Fred Rayman collection*

PD4501-149 First Baptist Church of Perrine. Perrine, Florida, on March 17, 1979. *Fred Rayman collection*

PD4501-164 was used in Charter service for Mans Bus Rental Service of Washington, D.C., on July 7, 1983. *Fred Rayman collection*

PD4501-452 seen here for sale in Stuart, Florida, by the First Baptist Church. This coach is currently undergoing a complete restoration back to the original Greyhound livery by Wilson Bus Lines of East Templeton, Massachusetts. *Ron Van Kleech photo; Fred Rayman collection*

Gordon Pfalzgraf of Belpre, Ohio, owns PD4501-536 and has converted it to a hatchback, allowing him to haul a car inside. Mr. Pfalzgraf was a very early inventor of custom fitted cloth car covers, and used his Scenicruiser hatchback to display his covers at various antique car shows. *Fred Rayman collection*

Howard Nash of Ventourus Charters owns PD4501-777 in Louisville, Kentucky. This coach was mostlikely the last Scenicruiser to be retired from private Charter service in the U.S.A., here at Shawnee, Oklahoma, on August 7, 1990. *Fred Rayman collection*

E. Lassiter's Bus Service #5 (PD4501-713) of Suffolk, Virginia. *Fred Rayman collection*

PD4501-574 was owned by California Parlor Cars, a wholly owned subsidiary of Greyhound Lines. X-64 was photographed in San Francisco, California, in October of 1968. *Fred Rayman collection*

A Tropical Adventure Charters Scenicruiser seen at the ABC Bus Company garage facility in Orlando, Florida, on Jun 27, 1983. *Ron Van Kleech photo*

Beaver Valley Charters #529 (PD4501-667) of New Brighton, Pennsylvania, photographed in Norfolk, Virginia, on April 30, 1972. *Fred Rayman collection*

Dawson United Methodist church (PD4501-893) on April 20, 1977. *Fred Rayman collection*

Domenico Bus Service #400 at their garage in Bayonne, New Jersey, on May 15, 1971. *Fred Rayman collection*

Eastern Greyhound Lines 4328 (PD4501-304) was later owned by Pentecostal Temple of Tulsa, Oklahoma, shown here on May 16, 1996. This coach is currently a motor home conversion owned by Dave Hartshorne of Hamilton, Ohio. *Fred Rayman collection*

PD4501-303 belonged to Glendale California Union High School, when photographed at Sedona, Arizona in April of 1980. This Scenicruiser is presently preserved as a seated coach by Jeff Wiley of Coggin, Iowa. *Fred Rayman collection*

Grove City Bus Lines #62 of Grove City, Pennsylvania, while in Gallop, New Mexico. This is one of many Scenicruisers that would eventually receive PD-4106 four-headlight system conversions while still in Greyhound service. *Fred Rayman collection*

Fred Rayman and his dear friend, the late "Sully" H.C. Sullivan, with PD4501-372 in Houston, Texas, on July 2, 1985. *Fred Rayman collection*

J. R. Hobbs Bus Service #1976 (PD4501-732) at "Kings Dominion" amusement park in Doswell, Virginia in 1977. *Fred Rayman collection*

James Brown, "The hardest working man in show business," as he was called, owned a Scenicruiser tour bus. PD4501-481 was owned by the R&B/Blues star throughout the 1970s, but photographed here on September 9, 1980, in Miami, Florida. *Ron Van Kleech photo; Fred Rayman collection*

PD4501-911 was used in charter service as National Bus Service #906 of Elmont, Virginia, on November 7, 1976. *Bruce Korusek collection*

PD4501-945 (N-86) belonged to Newton Bus Service of Newton, Virginia. This coach is currently a motor home conversion project, owned by Jack Hart of Hickory, North Carolina. *Fred Rayman collection*

A Scenicruiser owned by the Cavaliers Drum and Bugle Corps of Rosemont, Illinois, pictured here in Oklahoma City, Oklahoma, on October of 1987. *Fred Rayman collection*

Former Great Lakes Greyhound Lines G7275 (PD4501-598) was lovingly referred to as "Rosie" by its owner, country music star Hoyt Axton, pictured here in Oklahoma City, Oklahoma on September 10, 1983. *Fred Rayman collection*

Seymour Charter Bus Lines #587 (PD4501-840) in Knoxville, Tennessee. *Fred Rayman collection*

Kansas State University's "Continental Theatre Company" in Scott, Kansas, circa early 1970s. *Fred Rayman collection*

Former Eastern Greyhound Lines 4468 (PD4501-843) owned by Irvin Hoover of Mt. Pleasant, Pennsylvania, was utilized as a mobile hobby and wood working shop. *Photo by Santo Chase; Tom McNally collection*

Saddle River Tours of Wallington, New Jersey, #548 (PD4501-746) "SRT Casino Express" is seen here at Giants stadium located in East Rutherford, New Jersey, in the Meadowlands sports complex on September 24, 1983. Sadly, this coach was later destroyed by an arson fire on April 15, 1984. *Fred Rayman collection*

Trailways 182 (PD4501-745) in Tyler, Texas, circa 1982. *Photo by Joe Richards; Fred Rayman collection*

Continental Singers owned PD4501-975 when photographed in Ottawa, Ontario, in July of 1975. *Peter Newgard Photo; Fred Rayman collection*

PD4501-060 was used as charter coach service #502 by American Sightseeing Tours, photographed on March 28, 1976, in Woodbine, Maryland. *Photo by Bruce Korusek; Fred Rayman collection*

Chapter 8: Where Are They Now?

There is good news about the approximately 230 remaining Scenicruisers that survive today. People are turning their attention to the true historical significance of these buses. Enthusiasm and respect are building for their preservation. It has been noticed among the seasoned fans, that over the last 15 years a new, younger crowd is growing; some were not even born when Scenics were originally out pounding the pavement. This is an essential trend for the continuation of the Scenicruiser hobby. Europeans have a keen eye for mid-century American vehicles, and have imported approximately 10 Scenicruisers within the past decade for restoration or motorhome conversion. Throughout the 1980s, Greyhound located and restored several antique buses, including Scenicruiser PD4501-001. This is thanks to the forethought and dedication of Fred Dunikoski, former Greyhound President and CEO (1979-1987). This historic fleet is still owned and maintained by Greyhound, and is used upon occasion for movie appearances and promotions. Museums have also taken notice of the need for preservation. The Pacific Bus Museum in Fremont, California, is currently restoring PD4501-742. The Greyhound Origin Museum, located in Hibbing, Minnesota, owns PD4501-992. The Commonwealth Coach and Trolley Museum in Roanoke, Virginia, has preserved a pair: PD4501-1000 and PD4501-427. The Minnesota Transportation Museum, located in St. Paul, Minnesota, also owns PD4501-739. The Wheels of Yesterday Museum located in Ocean City, Maryland, displays PD4501-743. But these nearly-60-year-old vehicles are not just museum relics; several private owners have also taken on the challenge of restoring some examples to original condition. The unique, classic styling has become a favorite for motor-home conversion projects. This application lends a definite functionality to private coach ownership. There is no limit to the creativity and talent that bus conversion owners possess. Most of the remaining Scenicruisers probably would not be around if not for being repurposed as motor homes. For all too many folks of the past, they were considered "just another old bus" that should be scrapped when no longer profitable for revenue coach service. If one keeps a close watch where one lives, a Scenicruiser may actually be seen roaring down the highway sometime. Periodically, owners and aficionados gather to ride, drive, and celebrate their passion for their favorite old bus. Scenicruise 2006, as it was christened, was the first of such gatherings. Laughlin, Nevada, was the chosen spot for this meeting of six Scenicruisers for a weekend of fun and bus memories. The midpoint of U.S. Route 66, in the town of Adrian, Texas, was the location for the next meeting, Scenicruise 2010. A total of 10 Greyhound Scenicruisers were driven from all different parts of the United States to this "Hounds of the Mother Road Reunion." Devotees traveled from as far as Australia to enjoy this historic assembly of coaches. To see a group of these classics running down the road together in a group is really something special to behold. The 2011 rally was held at Grand Canyon Caverns, Arizona. A group of five Scenicruisers made the journey to this historic Route 66 attraction. "The Ghosts of Highway 61 – Dixie Tour 2013" will be a larger rally for antique coaches (with Scenicruiser emphasis) to be held at the restored art deco style Greyhound terminal in Blytheville, Arkansas, April 4-6, 2013. There is no official club or organization associated with this particular model bus as of yet. Creating a club has been extensively discussed, but at this time most owners tend to like the casual, loose affiliation that has emerged. The internet has helped this hobby tremendously with communication. Now, when someone spots a 4501 parked somewhere, or someone is in need of parts or advice, the whole world can be notified. The 4501 owners and fans are a close-knit group who are some of the most friendly, most helpful people one could hope to meet. The reproduction of rare, unavailable parts has become a community effort through the cooperation of many individuals. As a group, Scenicruiser enthusiasts do their best to save even the most derelict examples from the scrap pile, as it is so sad to see one lost forever. In the future, it is hoped that Greyhound Scenicruiser fans continue to represent a special group of friends who are making memories with their families, preserving history, and enjoying their hobby to the fullest.

PD4501-468 on U.S. Route 66 near Goffs, California, en route to "Scenicruise 2011" gathering held at Grand Canyon Caverns in Peach Springs, Arizona. This former church bus belongs to Tony Cooksey-Allen of San Diego, California. *Tom McNally collection*

Frank Gonzales of Pico Rivera, California, owns this beautiful motor home conversion (PD4501-151). The former Eastern Greyhound Lines 4241 Hartford Executive coach was photographed along Route 66 at Grand Canyon Caverns in Peach Springs, Arizona, in May of 2011. *Tom McNally collection*

Montpelier, Ohio, is home for Gary Pirtle and his PD4501-733 motor home conversion. This photo was taken at "Scenicruise 2010" in Adrian, Texas, in April of 2010, by Hari McNally. *Tom McNally collection*

Beautifully restored PD4501-083 belongs to Roy Hall of Rainham, in the county of Kent, England. The coach was purchased in April of 2000 in the U.S.A, was shipped to England for partial restoration, and eventually returned to the U.S.A. for completion in 2011. *Roy Hall collection*

Five old hounds along Route 66 at Hackberry, Arizona, for "Scenicruise 2011." Left to right: PD4501-389, PD4501-847, PD4501-082, PD4501-468, PD4501-151. *Tom McNally collection*

Jeff Willard of Silver City, New Mexico, drove his motor home conversion project (PD4501-847) to "Scenicruise 2011" held at Grand Canyon Caverns in Peach Springs, Arizona. *Tom McNally collection*

Red Bull energy drink uses their Scenicruiuser (PD4501-769) as a hospitality coach to promote their products at sporting and automotive events. This photo was taken by Hari McNally at "Scenicruise 2010" during an appearance in Amarillo, Texas. *Tom McNally collection*

Five Scenicruisers at Grand Canyon Caverns, Milepost 115, Route 66, Peach Springs, Arizona, in May of 2011. *Tom McNally collection*

PD4501-771 and PD4501-104 parked at the Rock Café on Route 66 in Stroud, Oklahoma in April of 2010. Built in 1939, this iconic restaurant is a roadside landmark. *Hari McNally photo; Tom McNally collection*

Tony Cooksey-Allen's PD4501-082 parked at the Supai Motel on U.S. Route 66 in Seligman, Arizona, in May of 2011. *Tom McNally collection*

PD4501-897's owner was the late Jim Osborn of Toledo, Ohio, shown here in August of 2011. *Tom McNally collection*

"The Tin Tee-Pee" (PD4501-054) is owned by "Uncle Willy" Bill Holt of Shingletown, California. Photographed in April, this Scenicruiser towed a vintage Ford Bronco all the way to Adrian, Texas, for "Scenicruise 2010." *Photo by Hari McNally; Tom McNally collection*

Former Western Greyhound Lines 8088 (PD4501-713), a once badly corroded parts-bus, had the forward 1/3 section preserved as a child's playhouse in Peoria, Illinois. Photo taken on June 25, 2006. *Tom McNally collection*

Photographed in 2008, this famous "hatchback Scenicruiser" (PD4501-536) was converted to haul a corvette inside the rear, owned by Gordon Pfalzgraf of Belpre, Ohio. *Tom McNally collection*

PD4501-389 belongs to Chad Goertz of Agua Dulce, California, seen here at the Hackberry General Store located on Route 66 in Hackberry, Arizona, in May of 2011. *Tom McNally collection*

Dave Hartshorne of Hamilton, Ohio, owns PD4501-304, which is currently a motor home conversion utilized to pull a 35-foot enclosed race car trailer. Photographed by Hari McNally in Adrian, Texas, in April of 2010. *Tom McNally collection*

Former Eastern Greyhound Lines 4247 (PD4501-025) is an older motor home conversion owned by Mark Robinson of Owenton, Kentucky. The coach was once utilized as a band bus by the Robinson Family Gospel, and Bluegrass Traveling Band. *Tom McNally collection*

Western Greyhound Lines 8028 (PD4501-826) was completely restored as a seated coach by the owner David Pagel, of Anderson, California. The project was dedicated in the memory of Robert Watson, David's grandfather. Here it is in Williams, California, on April 26, 2009. *Photo by David Pagel; Tom McNally collection*

PD4501-666 is owned by Krijn Blaasse of the Netherlands. In 2010, the Political Archive Foundation was created in the Netherlands to preserve over 40,000 hours of searchable audio and video files containing local and provincial council meetings. The coach was used on a national tour to create awareness for this project, and to promote political transparency in Dutch politics. *Photo by Krijn Blaasse; Tom McNally collection*

Jon Hotvet (PD4501-822) of Minneapolis, Minnesota (left), and Greg Bush (PD4501-104) of Tulsa, Oklahoma (right), at the Desert Hills Motel on Route 66 in Tulsa, Oklahoma. These coaches were among ten Scenicruisers to travel from all parts of the U.S. to "Scenicruise 2010," held in Adrian, Texas, in April of 2010. *Photo by Hari McNally; Tom McNally collection*

"Kyle Brandt's orphanage for wayward Scenicruisers!" Kyle lives in Greer, South Carolina, and has gone to extreme links to preserve several Scenicruisers in his collection. *Photo by Kyle Brandt; Tom McNally collection*

Four Scenicruisers parked at the Round Barn along Route 66 in Arcadia, Oklahoma, in April of 2010. This unique structure was constructed in 1898 by William Odor. *Photo by Hari McNally; Tom McNally collection*

Pacific Greyhound Lines K-2334 (PD4501-832) appeared briefly in Alfred Hitchcock's 1959 movie *North by Northwest* starring Cary Grant. This coach is currently owned by Martyn Besselsen of the Netherlands; he is planning a complete restoration back to the original Greyhound livery. *Tom McNally collection*

Former Central Greyhound Lines 1444 (PD4501-498) now rests in a Michigan salvage yard, shown here in October of 2005. *Tom McNally collection*

The beautifully restored Southwestern Greyhound Lines S-108 (PD4501-074) is owned by Ash Dovel of South Daytona Beach, Florida. *Photo by Ash Dovel; Tom McNally collection*

Tom McNally (PD4501-771) of Peoria, Illinois (left) and Pat McNeal (PD4501-516) of Baltimore, Maryland (right) en route to "Scenicruise 2010" in April of 2010. *Photo by Hari McNally; Tom McNally collection*

PD4501-869 shown here in Lafayette, Indiana, in November of 2006. The coach was recently purchased by Wayne Meadlin of Fort Worth, Texas, and is currently undergoing a complete restoration back to the 1962 gold stripe Greyhound livery. *Tom McNally collection*

PD4501-771 (left) and PD4501-054 (right) parked at the Midpoint Café in April of 2010, located on Route 66 in Adrian, Texas. The restaurant was built in the late 1930s, was once a Greyhound depot, and is famous for its "Ugly Crust Pies." Adrian, Texas, is the mid-way point of U.S. Route 66 (1,139 miles to Los Angeles and 1,139 to Chicago). *Photo by Hari McNally; Tom McNally collection*

Roy Crowl opened "Roy's" as a filling station and café in 1938. Located in Amboy, California, on Route 66, this iconic roadside destination is still open for business today as seen here in May of 2011. *Tom McNally collection*

Former Southern Greyhound Lines 5534 (PD4501-858) is a motor home conversion owned by Gary Perkins of Utica, Illinois, photographed here in June of 2011. *Tom McNally collection*

Tom McNally's PD4501-771 at Magnolia Mobile filling station located in Shamrock, Texas, in April of 2010. *Photo by Hari McNally; Tom McNally collection*

ABOUT THE AUTHORS

Fred Rayman was born in Marshalltown, Iowa, in 1941, and raised on a farm near Toledo, Iowa. Fred became interested in fire fighting at an early age because his school bus driver was a Toledo volunteer firefighter. He attended Oklahoma State University in Stillwater, Oklahoma, and graduated college in 1962 with a degree in Fire Protection Engineering. While in high school, in 1956, Fred traveled by bus to Provo, Utah, to visit his aunt and uncle. This trip would influence the rest of his life, as it was aboard not just any bus, but a Greyhound Scenicruiser! It was at this time that Fred began to keep newspaper clippings or any other Scenicruiser-related souvenirs he could find. After graduating college, Fred took a job with the Factory Insurance Association (F.I.A.) in Minneapolis, Minnesota, as a loss prevention engineer. He served in the U.S. Army (1963-1965) as a Hawk missile technician with permanent duty post at Key West, Florida. After the Army, he went back to the insurance business; however, after spending time in south Florida, found the Minnesota winters to be unbearable. Fred went to Oklahoma City and applied to several bus companies for work. Oklahoma Transportation Company responded first, and Fred was hired as a driver in 1969. During his time at OTC, the company had a pool arrangement with Greyhound, Trailways, and other carriers, so passengers did not have to switch buses en route. Fred would trade a higher paying charter run just to get a chance to drive his favorite coach—a Scenicruiser. He still remembers driving the last pool service Scenicruiser (Southern Greyhound Lines5462 PD4501-355) from Ft. Smith, Arkansas, to Oklahoma City, Oklahoma, on January 3, 1971. Fred was a very active union member throughout his tenure as a bus driver, holding positions as Legislative Representative, Chairman, Vice-Chairman, and Secretary. Jefferson Lines bought the company in 1986, and Fred retired in 2007 after 38 years of service. Oklahoma Baptist University - Bison Glee Club members refer to their beloved charter bus driver of 42 years (four in his post retirement years) as "Derf Namyar" ....Fred Rayman spelled backwards! The "mini-museum" memorabilia collection he has amassed, including his living room easy chair (converted to resemble the driver's cockpit of an actual Scenicruiser), is evidence that no larger Scenicruiser fan, or expert, exists anywhere!

Tom McNally was born in 1968 and raised in Peoria, Illinois, and currently works there for a consulting environmental engineering firm. Through the involvement of his father, Tom became interested in automobiles and mechanical equipment early in life. In high school, he ran with the gear-head crowd and began restoring Pontiac GTOs as a hobby. As the hobby continued (at one point owning seven GTOs simultaneously), he became somewhat disenchanted with the competitive nature of the national car show circuit. The McNallys had adopted two retired racing Greyhound dogs as pets. As a birthday surprise, in 1997, his wife, Hari, planned a trip to Evansville, Indiana, to visit the art deco Greyhound terminal. Additional gifts were a book about Greyhound Lines, with photos of several antique coaches, and a current copy of *Hemmings Motor News*. As luck would have it, a Greyhound Scenicruiser (like the one in the book) was listed for sale in *Hemmings*. Looking for a possible diversion from the car hobby, and after several inquiries, a suitable Scenicruiser was located for sale by Andy Henderson of Weedsport, New York. So at the age of 29 in the summer of 1997 (with no prior bus experience whatsoever), Tom bought former Western Greyhound Lines 8149 (PD4501-771). Following a fatherly-like crash course in double-clutching from Andy, he drove his new bus 800 miles home. Since then, his wife and son, Joey, have become involved in the bus hobby and are *very* supportive of this unique passion. As a family, the McNallys have attended several "Bus Bash" conventions, and traveled with friends by Scenicruiser on many family vacations. Tom McNally continues to restore vintage automobiles, and now his favorite bus—the Greyhound Scenicruiser. He bought restored former Tamiami Trailways PD-4104-3462 from friend and co-author, Fred Rayman, in 2005. He also owns former Atlantic Greyhound Lines A-2267 (PD4501-1001) Experimental Prototype EXP-331, which is need of a total restoration. Being a Scenicruiser enthusiast has provided Tom an opportunity to forge lasting friendships with a variety of folks around the world, and a chance to travel the U.S.A. in the greatest vehicle ever built!

Fred Rayman (left) and Tom McNally (right) aboard PD4501-771 at "Scenicruise 2010" held in Adrian, Texas, in April of 2010. *Tom McNally collection*